1 0   S T E P S   T O

Successful

Customer Service

Let's face it, most people spend their days in chaotic, fast-paced, time- and resource-strained organizations. Finding time for just one more project, assignment, or even learning opportunity—no matter how career enhancing or useful—is difficult to imagine. The *10 Steps* series is designed for today's busy professional who needs advice and guidance on a wide array of topics ranging from project management to people management, from business strategy to decision making and time management, from leading effective meetings to researching and creating a compelling presentation. Each book in this new ASTD series promises to take its readers on a journey to solid understanding, with practical application the ultimate destination. This is truly a just-tell-me-what-to-do-now series. You will find action-driven language teamed with examples, worksheets, case studies, and tools to help you quickly implement the right steps and chart a path to your own success. The *10 Steps* series will appeal to a broad business audience from middle managers to upper-level management. Workplace learning and human resource professionals along with other professionals seeking to improve their value proposition in their organizations will find these books a great resource.

1 0 STEPS TO

Successful Customer Service

Maxine Kamin, MEd

PRESS

Alexandria, Virginia

ASTD Press is an internationally renowned source of insightful and practical information on workplace learning and performance topics, including training basics, evaluation and return on investment, instructional systems development, e-learning, leadership, and career development. Visit us at www.astd.org/astdpress.

Ordering information: Books published by ASTD Press can be purchased by visiting our website at store.astd.org or by calling 800.628.2783 or 703.683.8100.

Library of Congress Control Number: 2009920428
ISBN-10: 1-56286-590-0
ISBN-13: 978-1-56286-590-0

ASTD Press Editorial Staff:
Director of Content: Dean Smith
Manager, ASTD Press: Jacqueline Edlund-Braun
Senior Associate Editor: Tora Estep
Senior Associate Editor: Justin Brusino
Editorial Assistant: Victoria DeVaux

Editorial, Design, and Production: Abella Publishing Services, LLC
Cover Design: Katherine Warminsky

Printed by Versa Press, Inc., East Peoria, IL, www.versapress.com

CONTENTS

P R E F A C E

Please read carefully because our menu has changed. Press one (1) if you would like to skip this step. Press two (2) if you would like to learn more about the author. Press three (3) if you would like to request that this book have an audio option. Press four (4) if you would like to continue. Press five (5) if you would like to speak to a representative who can give you the Cliff Notes or Reader's Digest version. Sorry, that was a wrong entry. Please go back to the main menu.

Although the above instructions are obviously written in jest, often the phrase "press one" conjures up frustration, stories about service gone bad, and emotions that range from disappointment to anger. In a book about customer service, it would be remiss to ignore that service is not always stellar, and that technological communication channels exponentially increase the ways interactions can go awry.

Nobody can dispute that it is annoying to be misunderstood by an automated attendant ("Sorry, we didn't understand that entry"); told to call back at more convenient hours for the organization, not the customer ("We are at lunch from 12–2"); or admonished for pressing "0" for help ("This is a wrong entry. Goodbye."). While the act of being cut off may not seem monumental in and of itself, it goes to the core of our hearts. We have been rejected in our attempt to connect. Whether it is on the phone or in person, everyone wants to connect at some level. This is the foundation of the human experience, of which customer service is a part.

Customers have expectations. Most of them are reasonable. These expectations almost always have a human element, whether it is obvious or not. For instance, customers expect that company officials care enough to make a transaction efficient and easy (human beings are behind the technology), or that face-to-face interactions are friendly and receptive (clearly interpersonal). Associating with any organization is an extension of customer trust: **"I have chosen you to trust, and I believe that you will take care of my needs."**

Trust involves an underlying assumption that someone cares. It requires that there will be a person up front or behind the scenes who is devoted to serving the customer in a responsible way that honors agreements and results in the customer feeling valued.

Top-level executives are responsible for establishing the vision and mission for a responsive customer service culture. Everyone in the organization plays a part in working toward the vision and in making the mission a reality. A well-known hotel's vision is to "make the customer feel at home." True to the vision, managers empower staff to do whatever it takes to make customers feel welcomed. Housekeepers, front desk clerks, parking attendants, and all staff members are empowered. They have a certain amount of money to use if on-the-spot assistance is required but not available through ordinary channels.

It Takes the Team

Not all staff members in an organization are fortunate enough to have dollars at their command. However, to piggyback on Hillary Clinton's concept of "it takes a village," it takes everyone in a company to accomplish the vision of pleasing the customer. If you are a manager, supervisor, coordinator, or any type of leader, your role is to guide and inspire your staff. You are the one who deals with customers whom your associates have done everything within their power to please. They look to you for the one thing you can do to turn the situation around. Then they look to you for support and recognition for their efforts.

If you are a trainer, your expertise is critical to your organization. By providing workshops, seminars, coaching sessions, and even brown bag lunches, you can reinforce the service your company expects. Extra service to colleagues is a plus, such as one-on-one sessions for people who need hands-on help in learning a new program or concept. As one who does not formally evaluate employees, you are often perceived as a safe haven. You can be an enormous formal or informal customer service provider.

If you are a frontline staff member, you are the showcase for all the hard work that has gone on in the background. You display your talents as well. You demonstrate the skills you have every minute of the day. You're right out there. Everything you do is an opportunity to excel at service.

For all team members to succeed, the support that is required internally is paramount. Many companies are now looking at internal customers first as the most important to please. If staff members are not happy, it's hard for them to engage customers and do their best work. Focus groups are a good way to find out what employees would like to see in regard to business practices. Leaders might be surprised. With all the benefits that may be envisioned, and all the changes imagined, the most important concern might be, "I wish my supervisor would say hello to me in the morning." Confirmed by years of research, this is actually a request that firms found prevalent.

Aside from the critical nature of support, employees often have great suggestions on how to improve service. Research also confirms that employees' opinion of a company's customer service mirrors what external customers actually think. For many firms, listening to employees has cut costs, improved service, reduced turnover, and increased profits.

So, it does take a village. *10 Steps to Successful Customer Service* is a book for everyone. Executives to frontline managers to maintenance personnel, all have contact with people who can and will appreciate great service. Whether you benefit from a review of interpersonal skills, or find a new perspective on how to make the customer experience a pleasure, the power to please is yours. This book has tips, worksheets, and exercises that can be used individually, in group sessions, or with work teams to keep the internal and external customer foremost in mind. Exercises are designed to provide insight regarding why you chose your profession, help determine customer expectations, and present ways to bring out the best in you, your customers, and your colleagues.

Working with the public can be rewarding. If you focus on the positive, you may find that you can accomplish even more than you thought possible. The goal is for you to feel good at work and to help provide a safe, warm, and genuine environment for those around you to feel good too.

May serving bring you joy.

A C K N O W L E D G M E N T S

To My Dad

This book is dedicated to my Dad, Jack B. Kamin, author of the poem on page 84, which he wrote in May 2009.

Dad passed away on June 2, 2009. He was an extraordinary man and a wonderful father. He will always be in my heart.

To My Friends

Thanks to my friends for supporting me in writing *10 Steps to Successful Customer Service*. Special thanks goes to Mimi Clark, my best friend from high school. Mimi is a crackerjack proofreader who made the process of writing this book fun, especially in the wee hours of the morning.

Meem, I can't thank you enough. Your friendship is . . . *priceless*.

I would also like to thank Brad Stocker, who contributed the ideas about being a good customer in Step 9, and who is always there for me with guidance and support.

Thanks also to Karen Campbell, Phil and Joan Runnels, Dr. Donna Goldstein, and Pam Aeppel, whose friendship, to paraphrase Josh Groban, "lifts me up so I can see the mountains, and makes me more than I can be."

I extend heartfelt gratitude to Aunt Judy, my best buddy from birth; my brother for his great hugs; and to the best Mom in the world—my Mom—for her enormous strength, patience, and unwavering love.

Thanks to Mark Morrow, former acquisitions manager for ASTD Press. I wish everyone a Mark Morrow in his or her life. In addition to being an understanding and patient editor, he is water in a desert: always a welcomed comfort as a friend and a professional.

Special thanks go to Belinda and Lisa, my editors. Their support and expertise have paved the way for this book to be useful in the pursuit of customer service excellence.

May everyone be blessed with the pleasure that comes from connection with friends, family, and service professionals. It's all about caring and connection—what all the people mentioned here have offered me.

Sincerely,

Maxine Kamin, MEd

INTRODUCTION

Imagine that each time you visited a store, ate at a restaurant, shopped online, or called your cable company, you were enthralled with the service provider. You smiled after you finished the transaction. You had a sense of contentment. You enjoyed the experience.

With the right mindset on behalf of the service provider as well as the customer, ending on a high note is surely possible. The reference to music is not unintentional. Just like a great performance by a jazz band, all players in a service transaction have to be listening, paying attention, improvising, and working together to create experiences that are "in time," follow certain rules, and are pleasing to the audience.

To continue the jazz analogy, musicians honor the composer by determining creative ways to play a song, and use chords and notes to guide their work. Similarly, service providers honor their company's mission, and practice improvisation by using problem solving and interpersonal expertise to guide their creative talents. All want to enchant their audience.

Most musicians enjoy making music. With the right instruments—tools—for you, you should increase the amount of pleasure that you get from creating harmony in the workplace. You deserve the gratification and recognition.

An Overview of the Book

John Naisbitt (1982), in his book *Megatrends*, summed up the essence of customer service. One of my training slides paraphrases the concept. His words are so powerful that most class participants stare wide-eyed at the screen, take a deep breath, and often sigh—because it is so true. Here's the slide.

> ## Caring Is the Greatest Gift
>
> *In these days of fast companies, desktop overload, and "Press 1" for service, we are all looking for a little comfort—an act of kindness to get us through the day. Caring is the greatest gift we can give someone.*
> *It is immeasurable.*

An Introduction to the 10 Steps

Each step in *10 Steps to Successful Customer Service* has caring as its foundation. You will have an opportunity to review your reasons for entering a field that requires such compassion and personal commitment. Whether you are a customer service provider, a trainer, a manager, or an executive, your enthusiasm is paramount to success. The steps in this book give you an opportunity to reflect on your personal service mission and customer goals for the organization in which you serve. The book will also offer ways to work with internal and external customers, and provide the reasons behind actions that are being recommended for optimum communication. Supervisors, managers, trainers, and leaders of all types can use the exercises to build teams devoted to service, and to discuss best practices. Suggestions on how to do this are included in the exercises.

Step 1: Identify Service Motivation and Mission

Most of us have to make a living. However, many of us who work in service fields have a desire to assist others in a variety of ways, and that is our main reason for going to work every day. It is a lot easier to work in a service field if you are devoted to it. Step 1 allows you to take a look at your skills and values, and how they relate to your personal mission.

Step 2: Define Great Service for Your Organization

Great service depends on a variety of talents, including those that have been studied by researchers, and those that your own customers require as measured by surveys, observation, personal comments, Internet responses, and other methods you use to determine customer satisfaction. Step 2 gives you up-to-date research on the factors that customers insist on receiving.

Step 3: Form Great Relationships

Customers form impressions almost instantaneously, most within the first four seconds of meeting you. Step 3 offers tips on making a great first impression by paying close attention to what you do from the moment of contact. The step also discusses reciprocity, and ways to examine the give and take of customer and provider relationships.

Step 4: Build Trusting Relationships that Last

From the first moment on, you are building trust. Step 4 assists you in examining how trust develops personally between customers and staff, as well as how the company builds trust. This step reviews actions such as listening and asking the right questions, as well as honesty in advertising and marketing.

Step 5: Use the Law of Attraction—Be Positive

The Law of Attraction says, "Be positive and you will attract positive people, behaviors, and actions into your life." Staying positive is a challenge in customer service, but it is the most important skill you can learn, and there are ways to project positivism that start interactions well and head off problems. Staying positive in phone communications and email is also important. All methods of communication count. Step 5 will give you information on how to turn negatives into positives.

Step 6: Aggressively Solve Problems—the Bigger the Better

Step 6 presents a Model for Problem Solving. The model gives a step-by-step approach to problem solving that will help you define the real issue and develop solutions. You will learn how to deal with complaints, appreciate your customers, and use the "Fantastic Service Equation," a tool that ensures excellent service in all parts of the customer service transaction.

Step 7: Recover from Mistakes Gracefully

Nobody ever intends to disappoint a customer, but it happens. Mistakes are made even under the best of circumstances. When mistakes occur, it's important to apologize. Step 7 conveys the importance of an apology, and the necessity to fix the problem as soon as possible to "recover" from the error. Giving something of value to show good faith is also explored.

Step 8: Give Customers and Yourself a Break

Customers come in all different sizes, shapes, and personalities. Understanding their differences is important to customer service. How you see the world may not be how others view it. Being aware of different personality types helps you respond in ways that foster understanding. Step 8 describes different personality types and learning styles and gives you ways to respond to a variety of behaviors.

Step 9: Keep It Cool When Things Get Hot

What pushes your buttons? What behaviors really drive you up a wall? Step 9 will help you identify what annoys you, for the purpose of allowing you to think before you respond. Button pushers often cause us to react. If you know what you are most likely to react to, you can stop an interaction from escalating. This step also covers ways to negotiate with people and diffuse difficult situations.

Step 10: Be Your Own Best Customer

After all is said and done, customer service begins and ends with you. If you're happy and satisfied with what you do at your job as well as outside of work, your emotional and physical strength will allow you to continue finding joy and pleasure in working with others. Step 10 provides suggestions for keeping physically and mentally healthy, and honors you.

Use the principles in the steps to make life at work interesting, challenging, and rewarding. *10 Steps to Successful Customer Service* brings you ways to enhance your work life so you can experience the success and fulfillment that comes with honing your skills and serving others.

Creating and Supporting a Customer Service Culture

There are systematic customer-friendly aspects of an organization's culture that must be in place to support all the hard work that goes into pleasing customers. These include financial procedures, customer focus, growth and learning, and business processes and technologies. Find out specific components of these categories in Appendix A.

Enjoy the Journey

At the end of this book, I have included a roundup of all the worksheets, exercises, and tools designed to help individuals, leaders, and training professionals find new pathways to develop personally or develop others to become great customer service professionals. Feel free to use this handy development tool and pick and choose among the many options to find the mix that is just right for your purposes and the service journey you wish to take.

Identify Service Motivation and Mission

OVERVIEW

- Your career choice
- Reassess and review skills
- Identify your values
- Create a mission statement
- Reveal hidden talents

If you are in a service field, you have chosen a noble profession. Your gracious actions assist people with services they need and decisions that improve the quality of their lives. For your part in interactions, working with the public can be rewarding and endearing. You know you have made a difference when customers appreciate you. Those are the times when you are glad to help and provide guidance to clientele who are friendly, happy, and satisfied. Then, there are times when you must wonder, *"What was I thinking when I took this job?"* That's when your goodwill is taxed and your nerves are shot. Your smile is beginning to wane, and the demanding and sometimes demeaning behavior of customers is getting you down. Ironically, that's when you really do need to answer the question, "What was I thinking?"

Your Career Choice

Your initial career choice had rhyme and reason. Maybe it was simply, "I wanted to work with people." Or, maybe you took an entry-level job and ended up staying in the field. Whatever your original motivation, it's important to reexamine your purpose now, find what excites you about your field, and realize what brings meaning to your work life. If you can rediscover the core values that anchored your professional choices, or discern the values that drive you presently, you can mitigate the stressful times by remembering your overall mission. By doing so, you can overcome obstacles and succeed in providing satisfaction to others.

For the most successful professionals, service rises to the level of a mission. Below is the story of Silvia Smith-Torres, for whom service is a way of life—a mission that she actualizes daily.

Silvia Smith-Torres is the vice president of client services in a child welfare organization. In addition to her daily responsibilities, she interviews candidates who are applying for the job of child advocate and will be responsible for the safety of abused, abandoned, and neglected children. The job is a tough one, requiring long hours. Silvia oversees just about everything child advocates do, including visiting homes to check on children and families, presenting cases in court, documenting all interactions, creating case plans, finding appropriate services, comforting children and their friends and relatives, encouraging all members of the family to abide by agreements—doing this and more while being on-call 24/7. Silvia describes the job to candidates with explanations and examples. However, at the end of her discussion, she always says, "This is not a job. It is a mission."

Silvia herself is the embodiment of the mission. She is available to 200 staff members at all times. Everyone knows that if they cannot reach their direct supervisor, they can call her. The needs of her staff, families, children, and superiors are a high priority. She gets pleasure out of helping. Those who do well as child advocates follow Silvia's lead and adopt the mission to protect children, embracing the great responsibility they have in ensuring that families get what they need. They really care about their clients. It is a hard job to do by just following rules and procedures. Caring is the ingredient that makes people feel a sense of pride and satisfaction. In Silvia's case, it can save a child's life.

What Is Your Passion?

Whatever your service role demands, work is as important to you as Silvia's work is to her. What is it that you like about your work? What encourages you to keep going every day and feel that you are making a difference? What are you passionate about doing? Here is an example of passion put into practice and believing that it can be done.

As Maxine Clark, founder of Build-A-Bear Workshop, recounts, you must "start by believing you can truly achieve whatever you set your mind to, no matter how monumental it may seem." As the company's "Chief Bear" says, most people don't do that. "They stymie themselves and their ideas with negative thoughts."

Clark grew up in the 1950s. As a child, her biggest dream was to go to Disneyland. As an adult, after a successful career in the retail industry, Maxine's biggest dream was conceived when she was shopping with a 10-year-old friend who liked Beanie Babies. Her friend, Katie, an insightful young person, remarked that making Beanie Babies must be rather simple, and said, "We can make these." After doing research and talking with more young people, Clark decided the kids were right, and that she could incorporate her own love of stuffed animals to form a business. Build-A-Bear Workshop was born.

Today, the business is publicly traded, with more than 400 locations around the world. Over 70 million guests have visited the stores, and with 750 full-time and 5,500 part-time associates, Build-A-Bear Workshop is one of the nation's top 10 toy retailers with annual sales of more than $450 million (in 2008). The delightful story of someone who really put her passion to work is described in the book, *The Bear Necessities of Business: Building a Company with Heart*, by Maxine Clark with Amy Joyner (2006).

Completing Worksheet 1.1 will give you an opportunity to reflect on your own passion and job satisfaction.

WORKSHEET 1.1

Your Job Satisfaction

Instructions: Consider the people, location, leadership team, facilities, and opportunities for growth within the job you have now. Answer the following questions.

Why have you chosen this field of work?

What do you like about your job?

How do you make a difference?

What are you passionate about doing?

What would you change?

Who are your mentors at work?

Whom do you mentor?

Reassess and Review Skills

Today's workers need skills that weren't even imagined 100 years ago. Present day futurists can't keep up with the speed of change, which is caused by technological advances and the social factors that accompany rapid growth. Change requires reassessing skill sets for workers at all levels, from frontline staff to CEOs. For frontline staff, basic computer knowledge has increased from knowing how to key (this used to be called "type") to being able to maneuver new computer programs that evolve at a rapid pace. "Must know Microsoft Office Suite" is assumed. New programs are being added to job descriptions daily. Frontline staff members need to have the ability to learn and use critical thinking. They need to work with technology that allows companies to keep track of a data-saturated environment, which is what most profit and non-profit organizations require. Essential skills at work are as much about learning and being open to change and innovation as they are about what you know or have learned in the past.

POINTER It's not about what you know, but what you're willing to learn.

Organizational leaders must recognize how to tap into the knowledge of their workforce. There is no way for any one person to keep up with all the information necessary to accomplish his or her job. Leaders need to increase their ability to "hear" employees, listen to different points of view, and embrace the knowledge that their staff members possess. To do this, they must be open to new ideas and design ways to solicit information, both formally and informally. They must also recognize the huge demands that technology places on their staff, and provide supportive ways to balance technology with human warmth.

POINTER Leaders need to "hear" their employees and embrace the knowledge their staff members bring to the table.

High Tech/High Touch

John Naisbitt, the futurist author who made C. P. Snow's phrase "high tech/high touch" renowned, has been writing about technology and the human element since 1982. His research is extensive, and his passion for the topic is evident in the book *High Tech/High Touch: Technology and Our Accelerated Search for Meaning* (1999). As he observes, the introduction of any new technology alters relationships and societies. Interpersonal relationships change as a result; we don't know all the ramifications, nor will we because of the rapidity of change. His take on technology and knowing when to use it and when to "unplug," is explained as such:

> It is recognizing that technology, a creative product of human imagination, is an integral part of the evolution of culture—and that the desire to create new technologies is fundamentally instinctive. But it is also knowing when to push back technology, in our work and our lives, to affirm our humanity. It is recognizing that at its best, technology supports and improves human life; at its worst, it alienates, distorts, and destroys. It is knowing when to unplug and when to plug in.

The "soft skills" in customer service are "unplugged." We will be looking primarily at interpersonal skills in *10 Steps to Successful Customer Service*. However, the steps will also address how computer-based communication influences customers (electronic interpersonal skills). Technical skills cannot be ignored, as they are a big part of customer service. In this context, technical skills will include keeping information accessible and up to date so staff can focus on providing compassionate service.

Creativity is another skill that is becoming increasingly important. Richard Florida (2002), in *The Rise of the Creative Class*, proposes that human creativity is the ultimate economic resource since new ideas and better ways of doing things raise productivity and living standards. The greatest gap in pay, however, is still between entry-level positions, including those in the service sector, and what Florida defines as creative jobs. The lesson here is that the future will require creative thinking in all jobs. The more people are prepared to exercise their creativity, think in new ways, embrace diversity, and discover creative solutions, the more valuable they will be in the workforce, and the higher their compensation.

Another point to consider is that economists predict service-providing industries will account for nearly all of the new wage and salary jobs generated in the next four years. With the growth of this sector, there will be opportunities for employment and for professional growth for services professionals. Now is the time to hone your skills!

POINTER

Now is the time to hone your skills! The future will require creative thinking in all jobs.

Consider the skills you use most often, as well as those you might not use, but are in your repertoire. Think of how you are creative; for example, developing new ways to serve customers, recommending qualitative measures, improving processes, facilitating teams, developing themes for social events, planning and organizing functions, or creating new forms and methods of capturing data. Worksheet 1.2 will help you define the skills you already have and identify others that you bring to the job.

Personal Mastery

In Peter Senge's (1990) landmark book, *The Fifth Discipline*, he champions "personal mastery" as one of the individual employee's most important contributions to the "learning organization." If you have a high level of personal mastery, you continually reexamine your mission and focus on what is most meaningful to you. As Senge notes, if people are not encouraged to live by their values and vision—to contribute their talents and gifts—they resort to simply "putting in their time."

Now that you have reviewed your skills, consider how your talents fit into what you consider important. If you are a hotshot

WORKSHEET 1.2

Your Skills and Abilities

Instructions: Answer the questions below and then talk with someone you trust about your answers. Ask them to just listen. See if you have any insights as you discuss your thoughts out loud. Ask the listener to tell you about additional skills you have that he or she sees. Have your partner fill out this exercise, and then switch roles. You both might discover hidden talents you can share.

What are the key skills, knowledge, and abilities that I bring to my position?

What are the skills, knowledge, and abilities that I bring to this job that contribute to helping others in the organization, including my team and other teams?

What are the "hidden" qualities I have that I don't think everyone at my organization knows about?

How can I use the skills I haven't demonstrated in a way that will benefit customers?

What are some of the ways I have shown my ability to help others?

What are some of my creative talents?

How can I use my creative talents on the job?

programmer, but you really want to be an instructor, or you are a representative and want to be a supervisor, whatever your age, whatever your circumstances, there's still time.

Identify Your Values

Values steer our lives. What we value is incorporated in our personal mission. Consider Mary's story below and how Mary determines values in her life.

POINTER

Values may stem from beliefs, but in order to become a value, you must act on what you cherish.

Mary is a bright woman who works as a sales representative. Mary identifies her top three values as harmonious relationships, her family, and service to her community. She is the office peacemaker. She finds ways to support her fellow staff members, helps on projects from the holiday party to United Way, and covers lunch hours for people. She is a favorite of customers. Mary manages to get her work done within working hours so she can spend time with her family at night and on weekends. If we were to ask Mary to write a mission statement, it might look something like this:

My family members will feel my support and encouragement so that each will grow and reach their fullest potential. I will use my talents to accomplish professional goals while assisting others in a kind, compassionate, and supportive way. I will make people smile.

Your values ground your mission statement. They are the ingredients that make up the finished product. Values may stem from beliefs, but in order to become a value, you must act on what you cherish. Louis Raths, Merrill Harmin, and Sidney Simon, lifetime values educators, define the seven steps to identify a value in Tool 1.1. Take a look at these steps and consider how you determine your own values.

TOOL 1.1

Criteria for Identifying a Value

In addition to your skills and abilities, all of us have values by which we live. Values guide behaviors that give direction to life. Values encompass beliefs about how one ought or ought not to behave, or about a vision that is worth attaining.

From observation and study of social and educational psychology, Raths, Harmin, and Simon (1977) identified seven criteria that constitute what they called a "full value." In order for you to do a litmus test on whether or not you really hold a value, all seven criteria must be true. You must choose a value freely, without coercion. It must be yours. In addition, you need to consider alternatives, such as other values that are similar or even different. You need to thoroughly think through the consequences, so when you practice that value you can anticipate the result, such as the effect on others. For you to practice your value, you need to first be happy with your choice and willing to let others know that your value is dear to you—something you cherish. And, finally, you have to act on your value consistently. Below are examples of the seven criteria.

Choosing

1. Freely

If you were in the Army and you were assigned to a position in accounting, but you wanted to be a pilot, you would not be choosing your career freely. If, when you were young, your parents insisted that you become a secretary or teacher because women in their generation generally held those positions, and you obliged, you would have chosen your career under pressure. On the other hand, you would have chosen your career freely if you took personality and ability tests in college, examined what you liked and didn't like, and then matched potential careers to what you felt was the best choice at the time.

2. From alternatives

Let's say that you did choose your career freely. You knew you were good at writing and good at customer service. You examined careers that required skill in writing, such as journalism, and you examined customer service careers, such as Internet customer service. You ultimately chose call-center customer service because it involved helping the public, which you like. In addition, this choice allows you to use your writing skills to solve problems over the Internet for your customers.

3. After thoughtful consideration of the consequences of each alternative

If you examined the educational requirements for your careers of interest, the financial considerations, locations for school, likely employment, and all the important factors for making your decision, you would be aware of the consequences of each alternative.

Tool 1.1, continued

Prizing

4. Cherishing, being happy with the choice

Once you chose your career freely, from alternatives, and after thoughtful consideration, for you to value your career you would need to be happy with the choice, not just so-so. Your decision would fit comfortably with you, and you would be glad you made the choice.

5. Willing to affirm the choice publicly

If you were a customer service representative for Harley Davidson, who valued your job, and you were to affirm your choice of career, you might wear a Harley Davidson t-shirt in public. You would be proud to tell people where you work. You would enjoy the job and the people who visit your store.

Acting

6. Doing something with the choice

It is not enough to talk. You have to do. If you value your job, you would perform in a way that demonstrated the value—with enthusiasm and commitment.

7. Repeatedly in some pattern of life

If you did work for Harley Davidson, there could be many reasons for your choice. You may value charitable work, and Harley Davidson has a lot of charitable activities in which you could participate. You might value financial stability and the company pays fairly and is stable. You might be a motorcycle enthusiast, a rider who takes his or her bike out often and values the outdoors. In that case, you are practicing your values if you spend time outdoors, chose freely from alternatives, and publicly affirm your love of nature. And, regardless of the whys, if you value your work, you would show up every day, unless you were ill or had an approved vacation.

As mentioned before, all seven of the above criteria must be satisfied to determine a value. The criteria, applied collectively, describe the process of valuing.

Worksheet 1.3 is a checklist of personal values. The exercise will assist you in determining what is most important to you and what values you hold.

WORKSHEET 1.3

Checklist for Personal Values

Instructions: From this list of values (both work and personal), select the 10 that are most important to you as guides for how to behave or as components of a valued way of life. Feel free to add any values of your own to this list. Rank the order of the 10 you choose from most important (1) to least important (10).

___ Accountability	___ Health	___ Recognition
___ Advancement	___ Helping others	___ Security
___ Adventure	___ Helping society	___ Self-respect
___ Altruism	___ Honesty	___ Serenity
___ Appearance	___ Integrity	___ Service
___ Approval	___ Job tranquility	___ Status
___ Change/Variety	___ Justice	___ Success
___ Competition	___ Knowledge	___ Truth
___ Cooperation	___ Loyalty	___ Wealth
___ Environment	___ Meaningful work	___ Well being (emotional)
___ Ethical practice	___ Money	___ Wisdom
___ Fame	___ Personal autonomy	___ Work autonomy
___ Family	___ Personal growth	___ Other _____
___ Financial gain	___ Personal time	___ Other _____
___ Friendship	___ Power	___ Other _____
___ Growth	___ Privacy	___ Other _____

Create a Mission Statement

After completing Worksheet 1.3, think about how your values guide your mission. Take some time to write down a personal mission statement. Follow the tips in Tool 1.2. It might take a while to complete the process of thinking about what brings you happiness and what you want to accomplish. You might say, "I don't have the luxury of doing what I want; I have to make a living." That's OK. We all have to survive. As Maxine Clark (2006) predicts:

> I'm confident that if you love what you do, you'll always find a way to make enough money to sustain you and your family. Even if you can't do exactly what you want, find a way to come as close as possible to living out your passion. (Clark, 2006)

One of the reasons for looking at a mission statement is to see how close you are to doing what you want to do. If what you are doing doesn't match your mission, you may

◆ consider other options (leave your job)
◆ consider how you can use your current career circumstances to better align your career mission by taking on other jobs or more responsibility
◆ focus on what you like about your job and develop a "glass half full" mindset
◆ seek personal fulfillment and satisfaction outside of work.

Reveal Hidden Talents

Bertrand works in finance. One of his responsibilities is processing mileage reimbursement requests. Most of the people in his company know him for his efficiency in making sure they get reimbursements in a reasonable amount of time. It's nice to be the money guy. Bertrand is quiet and does his job consistently without much ado. He's a capable and solid worker.

One morning, just about the crack of dawn, Bertrand was at his desk working. Some people are early birds. His vice president, Dipak,

TOOL 1.2

Mission Statement Tips

Instructions: Here is an example of a mission statement. Randall Hansen, webmaster of Quintessential Careers, has a one-sentence mission/vision:

> "To live life completely, honestly, and compassionately while making a positive impact on those around me."

Use any of these suggestions to create your mission statement.

◆ State what you want to accomplish.

◆ Describe what you want to contribute.

◆ Describe the "real you" or the person you want to become.

◆ Write down what you would like people to say about you.

◆ Start your thinking with, "My dream in life is to . . ." and begin your mission statement after that.

◆ Respond to, "If I could be anything and have anything at all, I would . . ." and begin your mission statement there.

For additional help in learning about and creating a mission statement, visit www.quintcareers.com/mission_statement_samples.html. The service is free and without obligation. In fact, the owner of the service, Dr. Hansen, is following his own mission statement by making an impact on the lives of those who visit the site.

happened to be an early bird too. Dipak stopped by Bertrand's desk to say hello and they began talking. Dipak found out that Bertrand was well versed in developing websites, a skill and interest of which Dipak was unaware. Dipak asked if Bertrand would like to work on a new website the company was creating. Bertrand was very pleased. The website had been in the making for four years. It was one of those projects that was pushed aside when other priorities seemed more important.

Soon after Dipak "discovered" Bertrand's hidden talents, the website was up and running, complete with text, video, links, and pictures. It is a website for children who would like to be adopted. Imagine—a hidden talent that could result in many children finding loving homes. You can see Bertrand's work at www.childnet.us.

◆ ◆ ◆

Put It All Together

To better understand your professional career choice in the service field, Step 1 provided an opportunity for you to reassess and review your skills, identify your values, create a mission statement, and reveal your hidden talents. In Step 2, the elements of great service will be discussed, including recognizing what customers want and understanding how to create customer loyalty through personal effectiveness.

N O T E S

Define Great Service for Your Organization

OVERVIEW

Recognize what customers want

Create customer loyalty

Understand the importance of word of mouth

Review leadership behaviors

After you have determined that there are solid reasons to be in your field, the next step is to define the elements of great service. This requires responses to the questions:

◆ What do your customers think is great service?
◆ What do your customers want?
◆ What creates loyalty?

Recognize What Customers Want

The answers to the previous questions might seem obvious, but they are not always apparent. What you think customers want may not be important to them at all. For instance, in the 1980s, leaders in some companies determined that it was critical for phones to be answered within a certain number of rings, usually three. Companies scrambled to have enough staff for phones to be picked up by the third ring. However, after extensive study by service firms, researchers discovered that customers were willing to wait longer for the phone to be answered if they received what they expected when the connection was finally made: courteous and efficient service.

Current research validates studies conducted in the past. Pleasing customers, in whatever terminology you choose to use, has been and continues to be the overall goal of great service. TARP, one of the most recognized customer service research firms, now uses the term "customer delight" to describe exemplary service. Delight is achieved when

◆ customers receive service beyond their normal expectations
◆ customers are "surprised" with pleasurable experiences leading to positive word of mouth.

Many books have been written with the same "take people by surprise" theme, evident in the titles: *The Pursuit of WOW!* (Peters, 1994), *Positively Outrageous Service* (Gross, 1991), *Treat Your Customers* (Miglani, 2006), and *Delivering Knock Your Socks Off Service* (Performance Research Associates, 2007). Surprise is all about delivering fabulous service using random acts of kindness. Refer to Tool 2.1 for simple ways to catch customers by surprise.

POINTER

Customers want to receive service beyond their expectations. They want to be *surprised* with pleasurable experiences.

Actions that produce **customer loyalty** (sustained commitment) are
◆ proactively providing information
◆ notifying the customer of new opportunities
◆ avoiding unpleasant surprises
◆ providing consistently good service
◆ creating personal relationships.

Create Customer Loyalty

People can be wowed in many ways. Just a greeting, such as, "How are you doing today?" could be a surprise and a pleasure. To capture the hearts of customers on a more permanent basis, an ongoing relationship is important to sustain the positive feelings that have grown in the short term.

As TARP points out, the behaviors don't take much time, but produce the longest lasting and most dramatic results. The following story illustrates how a few minutes can have a lasting impression.

The first time I got a call from a clothing store announcing an upcoming sale, I was totally astonished. The manager, who enthusiastically assists me in the store, called me personally to say that some items she knew I liked were on sale. I thought that was so considerate! I went to the store and purchased the outfits, on sale, as promised. I continue to shop in the store, and at times, just drop by to say hello to the manager while I am in the mall. Of course, I usually buy something.

The previous example of customer loyalty was a direct result of a manager proactively providing information (phone call), notifying the customer of new opportunities (sale on particular clothing), avoiding unpleasant surprises (price as described), providing consistently good service (had been helpful before), and creating personal relationships (participated in warm, friendly conversation in the store and on the phone). Mission accomplished. And it was simple.

The following are examples of staples that can be used to provide excellent service.

Staples

Staples are focal points for service. While they may be simple and often overlooked, applying these staples regularly and consistently will make the difference between mediocre and excellent service.

- Be friendly.
- Establish rapport.
- Listen to what a customer wants to tell you.
- Be especially kind when someone has experienced a loss.
- Provide information.
- Continually provide good service even in the tough times.
- Ignore customer mistakes.
- Bend the rules if you can.
- Tell a customer about a sale coming up or a new product or service.

Demonstrate Personal Effectiveness

Personal effectiveness creates a foundation for building customer loyalty. The Forum Corporation, another top-notch research firm, identifies the following areas for personal effectiveness:

- ◆ effective communication
- ◆ service attitude
- ◆ problem solving
- ◆ continuous learning
- ◆ integrity.

10 Steps to Successful Customer Service addresses these five areas of personal effectiveness. These themes will be recognized throughout the book. Topics in subsequent steps will provide ways to improve communication and problem solving, promote a service attitude, and foster continuous learning and integrity. Recommendations are provided based on a landmark study by Leonard Berry and his associates at Texas A&M University (Performance Research Associates, 2006). They conducted the original research for the long-standing, successful *Knock Your Socks Off* customer service series, which focused on the following elements of customer expectations.

Customer Expectations
- ◆ Reliability—delivering what is promised
- ◆ Responsiveness—doing it promptly
- ◆ Assurance—knowing how to do it
- ◆ Empathy—doing it with respect and understanding
- ◆ Tangibles—ensuring that buildings, surroundings, and materials are attractive

---

Recognize the Importance of Research

It's good to know why certain behaviors are being suggested as ways to enhance service. Research is conducted to provide a roadmap on how to excel, whether it's for the company's gain or for your peace of mind and enjoyment at work—both important objectives. However, as we all know from roadmaps and MapQuest, you can't always "get there from here" without being aware of the terms used on a map, their interpretation, and how to regroup when directions are erroneous. Following the steps in this chapter will provide you with the most direct route to get you where you want to go and lead you to your final destination of great service.

WORKSHEET 2.1

Your View of Customer Expectations

Instructions: Complete Worksheet 2.1 to gauge your awareness of what customers want.

Who are your customers? What are their demographics? _____
_____
_____

What do they consider important? _____
_____
_____

How do you know? _____
_____
_____

How does your organization define great customer service? _____
_____
_____

What do you think of your organization's customer service? _____
_____
_____

What are ways you can bend the rules? _____
_____
_____

What do you do best when serving clients? _____
_____
_____

How can you improve? _____
_____
_____

What did you learn about customer service expectations from this step? ____
_____
_____

Understand the Importance of Word of Mouth

One of the ways that businesses grow is by word of mouth. Word of mouth is the conversation trail of the service your company delivers, as well as comments about company products and processes. What people say about a company establishes and maintains the company's reputation and the likelihood that people will continue to buy or use its services. Latest statistics indicate:

◆ One satisfied person will tell three to four others about the experience, and one in four of those people told will take action on the referral. This is not taking into account electronic communication.

◆ Personal interactions have the most impact on customer opinion of the company.

According to John Goodman (2006) in "The World According to TARP," other summations of what can be measured include:

◆ About 50 percent of customers will complain to a frontline person; only 1–5 percent will escalate the complaint upward. An 800 number will double the odds that corporate hears the complaint.

◆ On average, twice as many people are told about a bad experience than are told about a good experience.

◆ More and more people have a degree of "hopelessness," and don't bother to even take advantage of free service such as warranties because of the hassle they perceive they will have to endure to get what is promised.

◆ If you help a customer who has had a bad experience, and you do it quickly and practice excellent interpersonal skills, that customer becomes more loyal than if the problem never existed (up to eight percent more loyal).

◆ The ratio of cost to win a new customer versus cost to retain a current customer varies from 2:1 to 20:1.

Pete Blackshaw (2008), in *Satisfied Customers Tell Three Friends, Angry Customers Tell 3,000*, gives examples and stories about how the Internet has changed consumer power. Anyone can say anything about a company, changing the nature of how many people are willing to complain or post comments about good service. Those comments—good, bad, or ugly—can be viewed by thousands of people, and "word of mouth" increases substantially.

Websites such as MySpace, SixDegrees, Facebook, LinkedIn, Twitter, and LiveJournal show us that the larger someone's primary social network is, the larger the extended network becomes. If someone posts a comment, thousands see it. Blogs, websites, and social networking pages make it possible to reach an untold number of people, inducting a new phrase into our vocabulary: consumer-generated media.

The following are some examples of traditional word of mouth versus consumer-generated media.

Traditional Word of Mouth

Customer:	"I'm here to pick up my prescription."
Assistant:	"It's not ready. We don't have it in stock."
Customer:	"But, I called three days ago to be sure you had enough time to fill it."
Assistant:	"It will be in next week on Thursday."
Customer:	"But I need it today!"

The customer walks out without the prescription, vowing never to use that drugstore chain again. She tells three other people about her experience.

Consumer-Generated Media

Contrast the previous dialog with a similar story on Planet-Feedback, the website Pete Bradshaw started several years ago (www.planetfeedback.com). Add to the scenario that the medication was for the customer's son, who had diabetes, and that it had been ordered for years on a monthly basis. For several months, it was out of stock. Because the customer was concerned for her son, she switched drugstores. However, she had to go across town for the medication instead of three miles from her home. To add insult to injury, after being a customer for three years, the first drugstore never recognized her when she came in.

Hundreds of thousands of people read this customer's story posted on PlanetFeedback. If just a fraction of the people who read the post did not buy from the first drugstore, the store's sales would drop. As it is, that drugstore's reputation is in question indefinitely for those who read the comments.

There are many online sites where you can read comments from customers about what they think of service and products. The following are some resources for reviews and information about a variety of goods and services.

- Nielsen BlogPulse searches 75 million blogs (www. blogpulse.com)
- Google Blog Search gives posted information by last hour to anytime (http://blogsearch.google.com)
- IceRocket searches blogs, MySpace pages, news sources, and YouTube (www.icerocket.com)
- Epinions.com provides ratings and reviews (www.epinions. com)
- CNET offers technical product reviews, with editor's notes and consumer reviews (www.cnet.com)

Review Leadership Behaviors

At the helm of all good organizations are its leaders. Forum research shows that leaders can increase customer loyalty by being customer focused, rewarding customer-focused behavior, valuing employees, providing vehicles for customer feedback, knowing how to increase customer loyalty, and providing solutions to meet customer needs. The following suggestions will help you explore leadership within your company.

If you are a leader, have each person on your team complete Worksheet 2.1 or have the team fill it out together. Do the exercise yourself and compare perceptions. If you are a staff member, fill out the worksheet with your perceptions, and then complete Tool 2.1 to see how your company fares with customer service leadership.

WORKSHEET 2.2

Customer Expectations

Instructions: **True or False** (Put a **T** or **F** next to the statements below, indicating whether you think the statement is true or false.)

_____ 1. Being friendly isn't particularly important to customers.

_____ 2. When dealing with you, people want you to make them feel good.

_____ 3. When interacting with angry people, it is important to first get your point across so they will understand what to do and calm down.

_____ 4. People don't expect you to give them your attention at all times.

_____ 5. Customers want to be in control of the situation.

_____ 6. Your body language and tone of voice account for 40 percent of how people respond to you.

_____ 7. If you are friendly and nice, it will not be as important to solve customer problems.

_____ 8. When you say, "Those are our procedures," 90 percent of the people with whom you work will stop complaining.

_____ 9. If a customer has a problem and it gets resolved, he or she still won't be loyal to the company because of the bad experience.

_____ 10. Price always wins out over service.

The answers to Worksheet 2.2 are in Step 3 on page 35.

TOOL 2.1

Leadership for Customer Loyalty

Review the statements in the left column. Describe how the behavior in each row is practiced in your organization. List any suggestions you would have regarding how you would like the behaviors to be practiced.

Leadership Behaviors	Your Responses
1. Top company executives are customer focused.	
2. Employees are rewarded for customer-focused behavior.	
3. Customer and employee experiences are inextricably linked; managers value customers and employees.	
4. Managers know what to do to improve customer loyalty.	
5. Employees are kept informed about business results.	
6. Managers ensure that employees use their skills to benefit customers.	
7. Nonfinancial measures such as customer satisfaction or loyalty are as important as financial measures.	
8. Customer feedback is gathered continuously in a variety of ways.	
9. The company constantly gains insight into their customers needs and provides creative solutions.	
10. The company acts on customer feedback.	

Have you ever . . .

- ◆ Written a thank you note to a customer?
- ◆ Called to say that there was a sale or special promotion going on?
- ◆ Let a customer know that hours have changed at your location?
- ◆ Sent a personal note about something you knew a customer would like?
- ◆ Emailed a thank you?
- ◆ Let someone have a magazine he or she was reading in the office?
- ◆ Brought in magazines for people to take home?
- ◆ Called to follow up on a conversation that you had in which you offered to refer a customer somewhere?
- ◆ Complimented a customer?
- ◆ Given a flower?
- ◆ Given a thank you sticker?
- ◆ Walked someone to his or her car at night?

◆ ◆ ◆

Put It All Together

To define great service, you must be able recognize what customers want, understand how to create customer loyalty, and interpret the research behind why certain behaviors enhance service success. The next step is to identify concepts that will help you form great customer relationships from the start. Step 3 will take you through this process.

N O T E S

Form Great Relationships

OVERVIEW

Explore the concept of reciprocity

Build the groundwork for reciprocity

Demonstrate reciprocity to improve service

Smile, listen, and be friendly!

So far, you have explored your personal reasons for wanting to be in the field you have chosen. You also know some of the universal expectations of customers, and you have thought about what your own customers need. The next step in the continuous learning process is to identify concepts about relationships that will help you please customers from the start.

The popular relationship book *Men Are from Mars, Women Are from Venus* sold more than 30 million copies. Most people are familiar with the behavioral advice given by TV host and author Phil McGraw, known as Dr. Phil. The notoriety that relationship counseling enjoys demonstrates the hunger people have to understand how connections are made. Human beings are curious about why people behave as they do.

POINTER

Human beings are curious about why people behave as they do.

Explore the Concept of Reciprocity

No one theory can explain all there is to know about social interaction. However, social psychologists do have insights into what some consider as the basic nature of interactions. One such theory is called Social Exchange, a set of principles developed to explain expectations in everyday communication.

In 1964, sociologist Peter Blau published the first version of *Exchange and Power in Social Life*, which looked at how people communicate. His concept of "reciprocity," still studied by researchers, involves people responding "in kind"—exchanging good deeds for good deeds and negative behaviors for negative behaviors. Other reciprocity principles include how much people perceive they are "giving" and how much they believe they are getting back. *Perception* is the key word. Except when it comes to monetary contributions, it is hard to determine who is giving more and who is giving less in an interaction. It's all in the eye of the beholder.

> ### Principles of Reciprocity
>
> 1. People expect that you will return positive interactions and that your actions will be of "equal value" to theirs.
> 2. There is an investment that is made in the giving of yourself, and the investment is expected to be repaid in a way that the giver perceives has as much value as his or her emotional "gift."

Theorists don't always agree on how reciprocity works in intimate relationships; however, they do agree that the principle is evident in the workplace. The following dentist's story is a good example of reciprocity at work.

POINTER
Reciprocity: People respond "in kind"— exchanging good deeds for good deeds and negative behaviors for negative behaviors.

I had a patient (we will call him Dave) who did not have a lot of money. When he came to me, his teeth were in terrible shape. I wanted to help, so I worked on him for whatever he could afford. I put crowns on his front teeth. Dave told me that it was the first time he had been able to smile in years.

One day, I was running behind schedule due to an emergency and I was late for Dave's appointment. When I was able to see him, he blew up and chastised me for being late. He told me his time was important, and that making him wait was inconsiderate. He was extremely angry. His attitude disturbed me because I am almost always on time.

Dave said he would never come back to my office, and I never saw him again. I'm not sure that I would have continued giving him the same discounts if he had come back. I was thrilled that he had been happy with my work. I didn't expect to be rewarded, but he could have at least given me the leeway on time that I had given him on price. It just goes to show that you can go over and above the call of duty and still get slammed.

This story demonstrates exchange theory and the give and take in relationships. The dentist would have been happy to continue treating Dave because he was being paid a discounted but fair amount and had developed a relationship that was satisfying to him. However, Dave did not hold up his end of the bargain and may not have continued to receive a break in cost if he had returned.

> POINTER
>
> Good experiences with companies are not cumulative. Each contact stands on its own.

The last part of the story brings us to the next principle of reciprocity. In customer service, exchange is implicit. Customers expect you to give them service and to do it with courtesy and appreciation for their business. You expect customers to act in a reasonable manner. Both you and the customer feel good about the exchange if it is conducted in a way that meets each person's expectations. If the customer perceives that he or she is giving more, even if the perception is illogical, there is an imbalance in the relationship. See Tool 3.1 for imbalance scenarios.

TOOL 3.1

Potential Imbalances

Instructions: Review the statements in the columns below. Describe how the behavior in each column is practiced in your organization. List any suggestions you would have regarding how you would like the behaviors to be practiced.

Customer	Assistant
Instead of the normal 15 minutes it takes for Priscilla to get to the passport office, it takes her an hour because of a traffic jam. She waits in line for her turn. When she gets to the window, the assistant says the office must close because it is lunchtime, and with staff cutbacks, no one is available to cover lunch. Instead of taking an hour off from her own workplace, Priscilla will now have to be away almost three hours if she wants to wait and fight the traffic back to work.	Jane, the assistant at the passport office, is handling all the customers on this day. She is overwhelmed, but doing well, until she is involved in an incident that seems to be blown out of proportion. A very angry customer explodes. She is yelling about the time she has had to spend trying to get her passport. She says she is going to call a commissioner. She keeps repeating that she is "giving" three hours of her time, and that she now has to wait until after lunch. Jane prides herself on practicing excellent service. She knows it is inconvenient for people to have to wait through lunch, and she was going to return as quickly as possible. The customer upsets Jane.

Staff Member	Manager
Kerrie has been working on a report for her manager. She has had several family emergencies that have caused her to be interrupted. In an effort to make up for lost time, she has conscientiously been working on her report at night. She has not told her manager, Bruce, that she is having family difficulties, nor has she told Bruce that she has been working on the report at night. When she gives Bruce the report, he says, "This is not what I had in mind."	Bruce respects Kerrie's work. Several days ago, he asked to see a report that he needed to submit to his boss the following week. Kerrie said she was working on it and that she would give it to him when it was ready. Bruce was concerned. He didn't know if she was on the right track. He decided to let it go. When she did turn in the report, it was not what he wanted. He was angry, but decided to do the report over himself. He told Kerrie that the report was not what he wanted. She seemed very upset.

In the examples illustrated in Tool 3.1, all parties thought they were "giving" as much as they could. They expected reciprocity as they defined it. Priscilla wanted to whiz though the line at the passport office since she had waited so long in traffic. This is irrational, but human. Kerrie expected a pat on the back because she had accomplished a task in spite of family emergencies. Jane and Bruce were caught off guard because they were unaware of how much their external and internal customers had "given" (in the customer's terms). See Worksheet 3.1 for more reciprocity principles.

It is important to note that all interactions are not give and take. Some are just giving. Some are taking. Reciprocity is not the same as altruism, in which, theoretically, actions do not carry any expectations of return. People can be altruistic and often are just that way. We will talk more about altruism and its rewards in Chapter 10.

WORKSHEET 3.1
Principles and Findings about Reciprocity

Instructions: Examine the research findings below. Write down your reactions to the statements. Then, examine how the principle affects your relationships with both internal and external customers. Managers can use this exercise with their teams. Use all the statements or pick out a few for discussion. As a summary to the exercise, ask the team to think of ways to improve teamwork and to compliment or praise colleagues.

1. Colleagues are more likely to consult each other about responsibilities than their boss; one receives help without exposing having difficulty, and the other receives respect. _____

_____

2. Most human pleasures have their roots in social interactions. _____

_____

_____

3. What causes pleasure to one may cause displeasure to another. _____

_____

_____

_____

Worksheet 3.1, continued

4. When a professional commands an outstanding reputation in his or her field, colleagues may be resentful because they are not being recognized as being as outstanding. _____

_____

_____

5. Some social situations are intrinsically rewarding, such as friendships. Friends find pleasure in associating with each other whether they are seeing movies, going to a football game, or just talking. The gratification is in the association itself. _____

_____

_____

6. The sociability in a functioning workgroup involves experiences that are intrinsically gratifying. _____

_____

_____

7. Most people like helping others and doing favors for them. _____

_____

8. One good deed deserves another. If people help each other out, they strengthen their relationship._____

_____

_____

9. A person who refuses to reciprocate favors is sometimes accused of ingratitude. _____

_____

_____

10. People seek the basic reward of social approval. Social disregard for others makes it impossible to experience this reward.

_____

_____

_____

(Concepts from Peter Blau, *Exchange and Power in Social Life*, 2008.)

> "Deposits," whether emotional deposits or positive customer experiences, don't necessarily build up over time. Each contact is a new contact, and years of success with a company or person can be eradicated by a single unpleasant incident—depending on how serious the experience is, and how the company makes good on the problem situation.

Build the Groundwork for Reciprocity

Worksheet 2.2 in Step 2 presented several basic customer expectations. The answers form the groundwork for reciprocity to occur. Meeting customer expectations up front will increase the chances for customers to respond in kind.

Answers to Worksheet 2.2, Customer Expectations

1. F   2. T   3. F   4. F   5. T   6. F   7. F   8. F
9. F   10. F

The following is a summary of the reasons for the answers.

1. **Being friendly is important to customers.**

Being friendly is essential to satisfaction. Problem solving is not enough. Customers want to be greeted with a smile, a kind word, a warm expression, and some social discourse that forms a "limited time connection." Even if it's for a little while, the connection will go a long way as the research in Step 2 demonstrates.

2. **When dealing with you, people want you to make them feel good.**

People want to feel good. They want your support and encouragement. Consider your own responses when you are in a customer situation. Let's say you are buying pants. Do you want someone to say, "You look awful in those pants. You need to lose some weight."? Or, if the pants aren't right for you, would you rather hear, "I have something that will really look good on you. Try this pair."

3. When interacting with angry people, listen to their point of view first.

There is no reasoning with an angry person. If you try, the conversation is likely to go something like:

Tom: "If you would only listen to me, you wouldn't be so angry! You need to listen."

Jim: "I don't need to listen to anything!"

Tom: "Calm down!"

Jim: "Don't tell me to calm down!"

It is important to listen before you try to make a suggestion or problem solve.

4. People expect you to give them your attention at all times.

Imagine a person with a cell phone in his ear, one hand typing on the keyboard, barely looking up at you, and saying, "May I help you?" How would you feel?

What is your reaction when you go to your boss with a problem and she says, "I can do two things at once."? Wouldn't you rather have her full attention?

Barbara Moss, Executive Director for the Florida Region of Kids Hope United, used to have a chair next to her desk. The chair was fondly known as "Barbara's Therapy Chair." When anyone in the company was feeling down, or had a problem, the person, no matter what level, knew he or she could go to Barbara's office and sit in the chair. Barbara would stop what she was doing, face the person, and listen. When someone was "in the chair," she knew that the person needed an ear, someone to listen and not to judge. She coached. She asked the person questions: "What do you think you should do?" or "What have you tried?" Before long, the magic of Barbara and the chair took hold, and the person solved his or her problem, armed with insight and usually gratitude. The coachee was able to return to work and be productive. People emerged from the chair with hope and a new perspective. What a blessing!

Internal and external customers expect your undivided attention at all times. They deserve it.

5. Customers want to be in control of the situation.

I was in a chicken restaurant. I asked for a chicken wrap. The server said, "We have no white chicken." I didn't know what kind of chicken was in a wrap, but I caught on that it must be white chicken. I was a bit flabbergasted. I just stood there, staring. I wanted to be in control of what I ate. I did not want a substitute.

Looking at my incredulous stare, the server said, "We'll have white chicken in about an hour. Can you wait?" She was genuinely sincere. I could see she was really trying hard to figure out what to say. So, instead of saying, "That's a long time to wait for chicken," I actually smiled because she was so earnest, and said, "I'll have a bowl of chicken soup. Thanks."

To work with a customer you cannot satisfy at the moment, be as understanding as you possibly can, recognize the disappointment, and try to turn the situation into one in which the customer can make the final decision.

> **POINTER**
>
> To work with a customer you cannot satisfy at the moment, be as understanding as you possibly can, recognize the disappointment, and try to turn the situation into one in which the customer can make the final decision.

6. Your body language and tone of voice account for 40 percent of how people respond to you.

Actually, it is as high as 96 to 98 percent when you include tone of voice. If someone stands with hands on hips, rolls his or her eyes, and says, "What do you want?", would you feel welcomed?

7. **It is important to be friendly and nice, and to solve customer problems.**

It is easier to solve problems when you have developed rapport. As you read in the research in Step 2, being personable and friendly is a customer expectation that usually yields results. However, if problems occur, it is essential that you work with the customer to find a solution. See Step 7 for problem-solving techniques.

8. **Explain procedures instead of just saying, "Those are our procedures."**

People do not like to hear the four words "those are our procedures." That sentence can antagonize the most patient among us. You can create a conflict situation just by mentioning procedures. People hear, "You're just a number. We don't care about you. We just care about rules." And everyone knows that rules are made to be . . . broken.

> **POINTER**
>
> People do not like to hear the four words "those are our procedures." That sentence can antagonize the most patient among us. You can create a conflict situation just by mentioning procedures. People hear, "You're just a number. We don't care about you. We just care about rules." And everyone knows that rules are made to be . . . broken.

Avoiding the words "those are our procedures," is not to say that you shouldn't explain procedures when it is necessary. Whys and hows may not always be well received when someone wants something you can't give; however, an explanation with a positive direction is more helpful. Instead of saying, "You don't have an original copy. Our procedures state that you have to have an original. You'll have to come back and wait in line," you could say, "I would be happy to do that for you if you bring me the original copy. That will show that you are the owner and it will protect your interests. I'll get you right in when you come back." See Step 6 for more examples of staying positive.

9. **If a customer has a problem and it gets resolved, he or she will be more loyal to the company if the problem is resolved to the customer's satisfaction.**

As research has shown, if you solve a problem, it is likely that your customer will actually be more loyal. When you solve problems with a customer, you connect. You appreciate each other. The customer wants to come back and see you again. You did something for him or her. He or she will want to do something for you or your company. The customer will probably refer others to you based on the great job you did in resolving an issue.

10. **Price is not always the bottom line.**

Some customers will always prefer price. Some prefer great service and are willing to pay for it. When economic circumstances are bad, we see a rise in people purchasing goods from less expensive stores. However, there are a lot of stores and many varieties of service. Poor service never wins out.

Demonstrate Reciprocity to Improve Service

Smile

You will almost always get a smile back. Try it anywhere. It is a warm gesture, easy to find contagious. According to Trainer's Warehouse, a trainer's organization, smiling also increases retention. When you smile, customers actually hear more of what you say. If your smile is seen by more than one, you may get more than one smile in return.

Just as giving a smile is likely to get one in return, the same holds true for a frown. Body language can be perceived as rude. If you are exuding "rude," you may get "rude" back without even knowing why. See Worksheet 3.2 for a game and activity on smiling.

Tips on Smiling

If you don't smile by nature, try these tips from Trainer's Warehouse:

- ◆ Practice! Smile at people! You will share a happy, friendly moment.
- ◆ Find a poem, a picture, or draw a picture of a fond memory and post it where you can easily see it throughout the day.
- ◆ Try meditating to relax.

Encouraging Reciprocity with a Smile

When you are walking anywhere—in the hall, on the street, or in a mall—smile at people you see. Notice their reactions. It is hardly possible for someone not to respond. Notice whether they react with surprise or with a smile. Try and think about what they are feeling—appreciation for being noticed, amusement that it is so uncommon for a stranger to smile at them, or another emotion. It's most likely that in some way, the smile will make you both feel good.

WORKSHEET 3.2
Act the Part

Instructions: This game is a form of charades. In teams, have people act out the statements below. This can be done in a classroom, at home, or as a team activity lead by a supervisor, manager, or director.

When You're Smiling, the Whole World Smiles with You

Smile 'though Your Heart Is Breaking

A Smile Is Worth a Thousand Words

Can't Smile Without You

Just to See You Smile

I Love Your Smile

Let a Smile Be Your Umbrella on a Rainy Day

If you would like to explore using other song titles for this game, visit www.songsets.net/words/smile/2.htm for 10,420 songs containing the word *smile*.

Nintendo has a face-training program that teaches smiling. The program is only available in Japan, where historically smiles do not carry positive cultural weight. However, with globalization and increased emphasis on customer service, this is changing.

In America, smiles are part of accepted and expected communication patterns. Since smiles are encouraged as nonverbal messages, most individuals smile when they are happy. Usually, a smile comes from within. If you can learn ways to view interactions as positive, no matter how they start out, you may be able to increase your ability to sustain positive feelings at work and smile as a result. (See Steps 6 and 10 for tips on how to stay positive.) With awareness, anyone can smile more often. It is a behavior that can be learned. As Nike suggests: *Just do it!*

Be Prepared to Listen

Listening is critical to all interactions. The first step is willingness. Are you willing to just listen? People who are willing to just listen have an easiness about their demeanor. They are "all ears," and it is evident. To be prepared, you need to clear all other thoughts from your mind. You need to "be here now." Be in the present, not in the past, and not in the future. How to achieve this will be discussed in the next step.

Appreciate a Thank You

You've heard the adage, "Don't kick a gift horse in the mouth." If someone gives you a compliment, he or she wants you to acknowledge the kind gesture by saying, "thank you." Many people feel uncomfortable being complimented. The following description of a conversation is common.

Kay: "Mary, I love your sweater!"

Julie: "Oh, it's just a rag I dug out of the closet.

Kay: "Well, it really looks nice on you."

Julie: "I gained five pounds, you know."

Kay: "It doesn't show."

Julie: "You're just trying to be nice."

Kay: "Well, gotta run. See you soon."

If someone goes out of his or her way to praise you, consider it a present. If you say, "I'm only doing my job," you will be invalidating the person who is generous enough to extend a kindness. Essentially, you will be discounting the gift. Responses that you can use after a thank you include: "It was my pleasure," "I enjoyed doing it," or "You're welcome, and come back!"

Be Friendly

My friend, Joy, was going to a new doctor. She wasn't thrilled about the adventure. Her trusted doctor of many years refused to continue to see patients unless they paid the $10,000 fee to be VIPs—so much for loyalty to long-time patients.

Joy entered the doctor's office with hesitation, wondering if she should just forget the visit, which wasn't critical. It was to establish a contact for a new doctor. Within a few minutes, she became resigned to the fact that she just needed to do this. After a short wait (surprise), she was taken in to see the doctor. He greeted her warmly and, before getting medical information, he inquired about a few personal details. "Do you have children?" he asked. It took her a while to respond; she was so surprised that he would care. "Yes, I have a daughter," she said. He asked the daughter's name and age. They began to talk, and within a few minutes the doctor discovered that Joy's daughter, Suzie, went to the same university his son had attended some years ago, the school where his son met his wife. What a coincidence that the children attended the same university! Joy was pleased that the doctor took the time to find out a little bit about her. Although knowing about a patient's family should be a part of any good doctor's intake procedure, the way his personal attention came as such a surprise illustrates how mechanical and unfeeling Joy had come to view the medical profession. She expected the worst and got a wow!

This doctor was recommended by word of mouth. We can see why.

> When people are weary, try a little tenderness.

◆ ◆ ◆

Put It All Together

It is important to focus on the principles of reciprocity and explore the give and take of customer relationships to improve service. Building trusting relationships, another critical component of customer service, will be discussed in Step 4.

NOTES

_____

_____

_____

_____

_____

_____

_____

_____

_____

_____

_____

_____

_____

_____

_____

_____

_____

_____

_____

Build Trusting Relationships that Last

Make a connection

Show you care about meeting needs

Listen on the idea and feeling level

Ask the right questions

STEP **4**

Building trust with customers can take a few seconds, a few minutes, or possibly longer. It depends on your role and your job. Someone who works at a checkout counter in a grocery store can build trust by waiting for someone to get that last minute item. Instead of saying, "You'll have to get back in line," she may smile and say, "I'll hold your place for you." Someone who works in child welfare, and has to visit a mom for the first time after her children have been taken away for safety reasons, may take months to build trust.

People offer trust in different ways. Some are skeptical. Some are warm and receptive. The time it takes to create a foundation varies from person to person. However, there are ways that you can foster the relationship that will help sustain it after the first encounter.

Consider someone in your life whom you trust. Use Worksheet 4.1 to list what it is that makes you feel close to that person.

WORKSHEET 4.1

What Makes You Feel Connected to People?

◆ What do they do that makes you feel like you can tell them about yourself?

◆ How do they respond to you?

◆ What do they do in terms of action?

◆ How do they make you feel about yourself?

Make a Connection

Some cultures believe that a person does not exist until they are acknowledged. That's an indication of how important it is to recognize someone in your presence. The following story illustrates how people wait to be acknowledged, and it also shows how important it is for leaders to be aware of how their actions impact staff members, even when they don't suspect it.

Brian was involved and committed to great service. He respected his employees and appreciated their hard work. One day, I was training his employees about the importance of greeting people. A participant in the class said, "But Brian never says hello!" That surprised me, so I asked, "Do you think that not saying hello is intentional? Do you think he's ignoring you?"

The answer was "no."

I continued, "What do you think is happening?" The participant said, "He looks like he's thinking all the time."

Brian was a deep thinker who always examined how things could be better. When he walked, he didn't always look around. I told him about the conversations in class. He said, "Oh, I never thought about that. I'll be sure to look up when I'm walking. Thanks for the feedback!" And he followed through by looking up. Employees were thrilled by his attention, and how he engaged them by asking, "How is your day going?" or "What's your best seller today?" or "I saw how well you interacted with that last customer. Thanks!"

The moral of the story: Say hello. You can learn about a company's culture by who says hello to whom. If people say hello to you, it is an indication that the environment is open and receptive. If nobody greets you, the culture may be less friendly or a hierarchical structure may discourage interacting outside of silos.

Listen to Show You Care About Meeting Needs

Building trust involves solving problems and having a passion for getting things done. Taking action necessitates knowing what needs to be accomplished. The only way you can truly determine a problem, or find out what the customer wants, is to listen. Many people cringe when they hear this. Why? Because everyone has heard it so many times that it seems trite. Unfortunately, we hear it more than we do it. See Tool 4.1 for tips on listening.

Listening is a gift, just like compliments are gifts. When you listen, you establish a connection that is real and genuine. You are the initiator of the reciprocity phenomena discussed in Step 3. Customers are more likely to hear you after you have heard them.

TOOL 4.1

Tips on Listening

Let the customer

- ◆ tell you the issue without being interrupted
- ◆ give you the whole story before you jump in and tell him or her what to do
- ◆ share emotion
- ◆ complain
- ◆ vent
- ◆ express anger.

One of the most important ways you can show anyone that you care is to listen. Listening involves putting your ego aside, not interrupting, and not trying to prove that you have the right answers. The customer wants to be in control, but he or she is not in control just by the nature of needing something from you. You hold the cards. Give some power back by listening.

POINTER

Listening involves putting your ego aside and not trying to be right.

Noise Gets in the Way

Behavioral scientists have studied how much time people spend listening and how it is done. For a conservative estimate, 50 percent of daily communication time is spent listening. However, most operate at only a 25 percent efficiency level. This is primarily because we think faster than we are able to speak, and don't always comprehend everything someone has said. "Noise" gets in the way. We are often

- ◆ thinking ahead
- ◆ preparing something to say back
- ◆ wondering how to get to the next meeting without making a rude exit
- ◆ worrying about work piling up

- evaluating what the other person is saying
- imagining what will happen if the stock market goes any lower
- fearing layoffs
- worrying about retirement money.

What did you say?

Listen on the Idea Level

The idea level is the thought level of communication. It encompasses what a person is telling you about a situation. It can be describing events or a policy. It could be when a patron asks if the library has the history book she is trying to locate.

"Listening" can also be done via the Internet. I was at the library trying to get the latest book by one of my favorite authors. When I accessed the catalog, I didn't find the author, even though he is very well known. I saw an "ask a librarian online" feature and used it. Someone from Orange County was able to "listen" well enough to solve the problem for me in the Broward County branch library where I was using the computer. But, the person had to "listen" very carefully, including clarifying my request.

Me: "I'm trying to find the latest book by John Naisbett, and I can't find anything in the catalog. This is odd because I have several of his books. I was just trying to get the latest."

Librarian: "So you want to find the latest book by the author you are looking up? Is that right?"

Me: (Ecstatic that he understood) "Yes! That's right! Thanks."

Librarian: "Was that John Naisbitt?" he wrote, spelling the last name correctly.

Me: "That's it. Sorry. I spelled it wrong."

Librarian: "If you hold on a minute, I can tell you exactly where you can find it at the West Regional Library if it is on the shelf."

Me: "Oh, thanks so much. I can take it from here. I really appreciate your help."

Librarian: "My pleasure."

Electronic "listening" and problem solving takes place in a variety of ways today, with technology issues, phone problems, ordering online, credit card problems . . . you name it. In order for a customer to be understood in writing, it is especially important to ensure that you understand. Paraphrasing is one of the most powerful ways to assure people that they have been heard. In face-to-face communication, it is essential. In electronic communication, it is equally as important.

Paraphrasing helps to decipher the actual problem. Even the most simple of transactions often need to be clarified. Think of a drive-through when someone is ordering—a live person is talking and a speaker is amplifying.

Customer: "I would like your mixed vegetable salad with oil and vinegar dressing and a bottled water."

Waitstaff: "That will be a mixed vegetable salad with bottled water?"

Customer: "Yes, but I want the oil and vinegar dressing."

Waitstaff: "Oh, thanks for repeating that. It usually comes with low-cal ranch dressing."

Use the tools you have to get it right the first time, and to let the customer know you care. Repeating back and paraphrasing are important. If you don't already do it, these two communication techniques can dramatically increase the trust that you build with customers, colleagues, and employees. And that trust is immediate. Following are some examples.

STEP **4**

Repeat

Repeating back what a customer has said may include introductory phrases such as

♦ "Now let me see if I got this right . . . you want to fly into New York, but leave from Boston?"

♦ "I just want to be sure I understand. You have been waiting for a supervisor for 15 minutes, and nobody has come to address your concern."

Why Paraphrase?

Paraphrasing is putting into your own words what someone else has said. The purpose is to let the other person know that you understand his or her message. It is also to give customers the added assurance that not only did you hear them, you understood what they were trying to say, and the meaning they were trying to convey. The paraphrased statement in the following story is underlined.

STEP **4**

> *"I was just trying to be kind," said Joyce, the young agent at the bus counter. "The lady was so sad. She was buying a ticket for the bus. She was telling me about her son. He was a doctor, and she just found out that he was in a car accident. I said, "**So you are concerned about the accident?**" "Yes," she said. "My son has a broken arm and lots of bruises. He will have to be out of work for a long time, and I don't know how he will be able to function because he is all alone." Joyce said, "So, there is no one to take care of him, and you are very worried." "Right," the lady said. Just then, a cell phone rang. Nobody answered it. It sounded like it came from the woman's purse. Joyce asked if it was hers. The woman then realized that she had a cell phone her daughter had given her, but she didn't know how to use it. "I don't know how to use this!" she said. Joyce responded, "**I know they are difficult to figure out if you have never used one.** I'll answer it for you if you'd like."*

It turned out that it was the son calling to say he had hired a nurse to care for him, and he was sure he would be able to return to work shortly. After talking with her son, the woman said, "Thank you so much for being here and for listening to me. It meant so much."

Empathize

In the previous story, examples of empathizing are in bold. The heart-felt "thank you" from the woman at the bus station shows the effect that a few minutes of genuine caring, demonstrated by empathy and listening, can create.

Empathizing involves feelings. We have feelings all the time, but we're not always adept at talking about them or identifying them by name. The following are some feelings that you might recognize from customers and ways you might validate their feelings by addressing them:

- **Anger:** I can hear that you're angry about . . .
- **Disappointment:** You must be disappointed that the item didn't come in yet.
- **Frustration:** It must have been frustrating to be transferred all those times.
- **Satisfaction:** I'm so glad that you are satisfied with the resolution.
- **Appreciation:** Thanks for letting me know that you appreciated my call. I'm glad you were able to get to the sale.

See Worksheet 4.2 for practice in identifying feelings. See Worksheet 4.3 for practice in paraphrasing.

Assess Your Listening Skills

After you have completed Worksheets 4.2 and 4.3, fill out the Noise Detector Assessment in Worksheet 4.4 to check your listening skills, identify your strengths, and determine ways that you can improve your listening skills.

WORKSHEET 4.2

Feelings Inventory

Instructions: Make a list of all the kinds of feelings you think customers could be having in your business environment. Making a list will help you be more aware of how to validate customers' feelings. Make a list of internal customer feelings.

Examples:

Customer	You—You are the Boss	Internal Customer—You are the Staff Member
Discouraged	Unhappy	Threatened
Pleased	Glad	Relieved
Frustrated	Anxious	Hesitant
Hopeful	Inquisitive	Expectant
Angry	Upset	Hurt
Delighted	Delighted	Delighted

Ask the Right Questions

Questions aid in obtaining pertinent information. There are several types of questions that can be used to elicit information. When you ask questions, it is usually most effective to vary the types of questions you ask so you do not sound like you are interrogating a witness. Questions should have a purpose. Let the customer know the purpose of your questions. Following are several types of questions you can use.

WORKSHEET 4.3

Listening on Both Levels

Instructions: Paraphrase the following statements and follow up with statements of empathy.

I do not feel like my suggestions are appreciated. Everyone says they would like to hear new and innovative ideas, but when I present recommendations, people are too busy to listen.

Paraphrase: _____

_____

_____

_____

Empathize: _____

_____

_____

_____

I can't believe I have been waiting in line for ten minutes, and now you are closing this counter. Do you have any idea how hard it was for me to get here? I had to crawl through traffic at ten miles an hour because of the construction on the highway and now you're closing. How can you do that?

Paraphrase: _____

_____

_____

_____

Empathize: _____

_____

_____

_____

WORKSHEET 4.4

Noise Detector Assessment

Circle the number that applies to you.	I Do This Well	I Do This Fairly Well	I Could Improve	I Could Definitely Improve
1. I listen well to people who have different accents and ethnic backgrounds.	1	2	3	4
2. I welcome interactions with people who have values that are different than mine.	1	2	3	4
3. When I am tired, I make an extra effort to listen to others.	1	2	3	4
4. When people are shouting or being aggressive, I listen carefully to determine their message.	1	2	3	4
5. When someone is sarcastic, I ask questions to find out what he or she is thinking.	1	2	3	4
6. I am eager to work through misunderstandings when they arise.	1	2	3	4
7. I listen to others with full attention, regardless of the topic or my interest in the discussion.	1	2	3	4
8. I make a conscious effort to paraphrase.	1	2	3	4
9. I listen to all of what a person has to say before I draw conclusions.	1	2	3	4
10. I let people finish their sentences.	1	2	3	4

STEP 4

continued on next page

	I Do This Well	I Do This Fairly Well	I Could Improve	I Could Definitely Improve
11. When I am upset or anxious, I put my concerns aside to be there for others.	1	2	3	4
12. I tune out all distractions when I am listening.	1	2	3	4
13. I acknowledge people's feelings.	1	2	3	4
14. Others know that I am interested in what they are saying by my body language.	1	2	3	4
15. I remain silent to allow others to finish their thoughts.	1	2	3	4

Scoring

How many of the following did you record?

1s _____	2s _____	3s _____	4s _____
List Question #s:	List Question #s:	List Question #s:	List Question #s:

What are some ways you could improve in the areas that you would like to grow?

_____

_____

_____

_____

_____

_____

Open- and Closed-Ended Questions

You can use open- or closed-ended questions to help you clarify or define a situation. Closed-ended questions are worded to solicit a short, quick, yes or no type answer.

Examples:
- Did you receive the merchandise?
- Did you order online?
- Were you at home when the delivery came?
- Can you bring in the receipt?
- Would you mind speaking with a supervisor?
- Did you call last night?
- Do you have your ticket?

Open-ended questions are used to obtain additional information. Open-ended questions require longer, more detailed answers and provide you with more facts, information, or feelings in the situation you are addressing.

Open-ended questions may begin with:
- Can you tell me more about . . . ?
- What else . . . ?
- What happened . . . ?
- How did . . . ?
- What would happen if . . . ?

Which questions you use depends on the circumstance—and whether you want to control the information you are receiving, whether you want more information, or whether you have the time for elaboration. Asking an open-ended question, such as, "What happened?" could give you information you did not originally have, and could influence how you view the situation. It also gives customers and associates an opportunity to describe their perception of the situation or conflict. A closed-ended question could give you information that you do not need to expand on.

Defining Questions

These questions help people focus on a solution. They are some-times considered safe questions that allow the customer to gain perspective. Defining questions provide a video replay of how and under what circumstances the problem occurred.

Examples:
- Under what circumstances is this likely to occur?
- When this happens, what do you do?
- What are the positives for you in continuing to buy this product?
- What changes should be made within the company to assure the best customer service?
- How often do policy and systems issues impact your service?
- How did you handle the situation?

Relay Question

The relay question bounces the question back to the one who origi-nally asked it: "What do you think?" This is a good way to involve customers in decision making when the solution requires coopera-tion. It is also excellent for coaching, as discussed in the example of "Barbara's Chair." If colleagues or employees need to talk through a problem, asking what they think is a way of helping them discov-er answers on their own. You act as a sounding board. Using relay and open-ended questions can build trust by demonstrating your faith in the person's ability to solve his or her own problem.

Past Success

In these questions, you focus on the customer's past successes with your services. Examples include:
- I see that you have shopped with us before. How did you perceive service in the past?
- What can we do for you to continue the relationship we have established?

- What would it take for us to regain your confidence?
- Tell me about the service provider you liked so much.

Scaling Questions

Scaling questions make complex features of a customer's experience more concrete. Scaling questions can be used to prioritize the customer's perception of hopefulness. They usually take the form of asking the person to give a number from 1 to 10 that best represents the severity of their problem, with 10 at the positive end of the scale. Higher numbers are equated with more positive outcomes or experiences. Examples of scaling questions include:

- On a scale of 1 to 10, with 10 meaning you have every confidence that this problem can be solved, and 1 meaning that you have no confidence at all, where do you see yourself today?
- On the same scale, how hopeful are you that this problem can be resolved?

See Tool 4.2 for more on questioning.

Trust Starts Within Your Own Company

Trust is a big topic. The suggestions provided so far are for you to begin to establish trust with a customer. In order to maintain trust, you have to be consistent with the excellent service you provide, and the company you work for needs to consider building trust as a critical factor in its mission, goals, objectives, and practice.

Trust as an Organizational Value

Your company must hold the following principles as sacred:

- **All business actions and interactions must be honest.**
  This means that the company advertises and promises what it delivers. If a car dealership runs an ad that says,

TOOL 4.2

Questioning

Questions are a form of control. When you ask a question, you are controlling the direction in which the conversation will go. Wait until the person has thoroughly explained a situation or talked through a problem before you ask a question. It is important to wait when

- someone is trying to tell you something or is describing an incident
- a person is telling you how he or she feels
- you have asked a question and the person is answering
- the person has paused to think
- the person gives you the verbal or nonverbal message that he or she feels like you are interrogating them
- you will take the customer off track from what he or she wants to tell you.

What should you do? Just listen. Your questions will most likely be answered if you give the customer the respect he or she deserves to tell you what happened. When the story is done, you can ask appropriate questions or begin problem solving.

"$3,000 off new autos," it shouldn't be just the test vehicles on the lot. If a hotel touts "best service," upper management, the waitstaff, check-in staff, bellhops, and sanitation staff should know that their service is included.

If you say you will be back in a minute, make it a minute. If you need to check with your supervisor to see if you can waive a procedure, give the customer a timeframe in which to expect an answer. Customers will usually wait and will often be much more patient if you tell them the truth.

POINTER

If you say that you will be back in a minute, make it a minute. If you need to check with your supervisor to see if you can waive a procedure, give the customer a timeframe in which to expect an answer. Customers will usually wait and will often be much more patient if you tell them the truth.

◆ **You must be a part of the solution.** Support your company by being part of it and taking responsibility. Be honest about a problem (such as the computers are down, you are moving, or you are out of that color shirt), but provide a solution if you can, "I'll call you when the computers come back up," "I'll get that information for you as soon as I unpack the boxes tomorrow," or "I can backorder that shirt for you, or would you like to try another color?" Avoid statements that separate you from your organization, such as, "They can't get the phones working."

◆ **Products must work.** There are a lot of gadgets on the market, as well as many high-ticket items. People are wary of brands they don't recognize, but they sometimes want to purchase new items for price, variety, or simply because they want to be one of the first to try a product. Make sure your products work. If you key in "products that don't work" on Google, you will get results about many products that consumers have found defective. The sites listed in Step 2 will also yield a variety of results.

◆ ◆ ◆

Put It All Together

From the first moment you come in contact with a customer, you are building trust. Step 4 examined how trust develops personally between customers and staff, as well as how companies build trust. Step 5 will focus on the importance of staying positive, even in challenging customer service situations.

N O T E S

_____

_____

_____

_____

_____

_____

_____

_____

_____

_____

_____

_____

_____

_____

_____

_____

_____

_____

_____

_____

Use the Law of Attraction—Be Positive

STEP **5**

OVERVIEW

Understand the Law of Attraction

Stay positive

Avoid negative triggers

Use positive regard on the phone and in email

A lot has been written about the importance of being positive. The Law of Attraction is a concept that has been traced through history from Shakespeare, Newton, Edison, and Einstein, to Jerry and Esther Hicks, Jack Canfield, Wayne Dyer, and many other popular psychologists and speakers.

Understand the Law of Attraction

The Law of Attraction is a principle that suggests you are attracting what you have in your life. Proponents of the concept teach that it is the power of thought that makes things happen, as if you were shaping your destiny one thought at a time. The Law of Attraction goes beyond behavior—to reciprocity, altruism, or other concepts of exchange or giving. It applies to what we actually think. Key principles of the Law of Attraction include:

Like attracts like. As you think a thought, you are attracting the same kinds of energy.

This holds true for attracting both positive and negative energy. Have you ever focused on something that was bothering you, and it got worse and worse, seemingly with no solution in sight? Then, when you let it go, stopped thinking about it, and changed the thought to "it will get better," did it?

Picture the following scenario.

Yari is disenfranchised because he bought a computer that gives him more error messages and aggravation than his sixth-grade teacher. He has come to Top Buy to return the computer. He approaches Jerome, a salesperson in the store.

Jerome is an efficient salesperson. He senses that Yari is angry, so he prepares for the fight. When Yari approaches, Jerome does not smile and greet him. He just looks at him. He is expecting an argument.

Yari begins the conversation by saying, "I need to return this computer. There seems to be something wrong with the operating system."

Jerome, thinking that Yari is trying to get away with getting a new computer and annoyed by what he perceives as impudence, barks, "How do you know it's not user error?"

The interaction escalates, and a manger has to intervene.

After the altercation, Jerome is angry. His sense of order has been upset. He says to himself, "All customers are like this. They are ungrateful and discourteous, wanting to take advantage of hard working people like me."

That day, several customers come to Jerome's station with items to return. He treats them the way he sees them—the way he thinks about them. He has quite a bad day.

The more you think a thought, the more similar thoughts will come into your consciousness.

Have you ever gone down any of these paths?
◆ I don't like it here.
◆ Nobody knows what they are doing.

- Nobody cares.
- It's a far cry from the way things used to be.
- Look at our world.
- Our politicians don't even know what to do.
- We're all at war.
- This will never end.

You could really go into a downward spiral if you continue this thought pattern, which is less than uplifting.

The same thing happens with thoughts about people. If you are negative, you will attract negativity. If you are positive, you will attract positivity. This may not be true 100 percent of the time. But, you can be assured that if you are positive, you will get a lot more positive energy back. If you focus your thoughts on what you want, you are more likely to get it.

The Law of Attraction doesn't compute "don't," "not," "no," or any other negative words.

Don't wish for customers who don't talk back, bosses who don't criticize, and colleagues who don't gossip.

Read that sentence again. According to the Law of Attraction, what will you get? (You will get customers who talk back, bosses who criticize, and colleagues who gossip.)

The same law applies to how you think about yourself. If you think the following positive thoughts, you will project those thoughts to others who will treat you accordingly. Most important, you will feel good about yourself, which is invaluable. That is really the key.

- I am capable.
- I can solve this.
- I am good at what I do.
- I like who I am.

Stay Positive

Use Positive Language

In line with the Law of Attraction, turning a bad situation into a good one can be as easy as telling a customer what you can do instead of what you can't do.

Using positive language is an art. It involves concentrating on how you communicate. In positive communication, you don't blame, you solve. For example:

Example: You didn't fill the form out properly.

Better: Let me help you with a few sections so this can be processed as quickly as possible.

See Tool 5.1 for more examples. Refer to Worksheet 5.1 to make your own positive language chart.

Avoid Negative Triggers

There are some phrases and words that are immediate triggers for negative responses.

POINTER

When you say, "No, you can't do that," even a small child has an immediate response: "Yes, I can." No is a strong word that carries emotion with it. There are few times when "no" makes you feel good.

Find an alternative to "no."

When you say, "No, you can't do that," even a small child has an immediate response: *"Yes, I can." No* is a strong word that carries emotion with it. There are few times when "no" makes you feel good.

Try not saying no at all for a day or two. It might be difficult, and you might have to end up saying it, but you'll come up with alternatives. It isn't easy. But, it's worth the time and effort.

TOOL 5.1

Positive Language

External Customers

Negative	Positive
"If your order didn't arrive, it's probably because you didn't key in the information you were asked to include online."	"Let me check on that for you. I'm sure we can find out what happened."
"Who told you that? Well, he was wrong."	"Let me tell you how it works. I can clarify that information for you."
"Didn't you read the sign? This is the wrong department for that concern."	"This is accounting. I'll call purchasing for you, and I'm sure they'll be able to get what you need. I'll tell you who you can see there."
"No, we don't do that sort of thing here. We're not community services."	"I know where you can go for first-time homeowner's benefits. It's across the street. I'll give you the address. There's a parking lot adjacent to the building."
"You should have come earlier. We close at 4:30."	"We still have five minutes until closing. If you're looking for couches and you see one you like, I'll put a hold on it for you until tomorrow morning."
"We can't fix your equipment unless you have your serial number."	"The serial number is on the bottom right of the equipment. We can get started as soon as I have it."
"That's the policy. If you call before 3:00, we can process your request the same day. It's now 3:05."	"This will be done first thing in the morning. I'll see to it personally. The credit will appear on your statement by the end of the day tomorrow."
"That's not my job. They handle that in customer service."	"I'd be glad to direct you to where you need to go to get your problem resolved."

continued on next page

STEP **5**

Internal Customers—Colleagues

Negative	Positive
"I don't have time to answer your questions now."	"I'll be over in five minutes. I just have to finish this up."
"You don't need to know that. Just do your job."	"It's good that you want to know the reasons. I'll explain."
"Why are you always late with the information I need? It holds me up with customers."	"I really need that information so I can work with the customers."
"I can't get the answers I need. I want to finish this assignment for you, but to do that, I need more information."	"Maybe together we can figure out who might be able to help you."
"You're new here? Lots of luck. We all had to learn the hard way."	"I can show you the ropes. We were all new once!"
"You're never at your desk. We have to pick up the slack answering your department's questions when we don't even know the answers."	"We need some way to be able to answer customer questions when you aren't here. How can we handle the requests?"

WORKSHEET 5.1

Negative to Positive

Instructions: Make your own positive language chart like the one in Tool 5.1. Turn negative statements into positive ones.

Sometimes I state things in negative terms:	I could say:

If you don't know, find out.

"I don't know" is not an acceptable answer if you leave it at that. Customers want to know that you will try to get an answer, even if you don't have one at the time. Instead of saying, "I don't know," be positive about what you can find out. Use phrases such as

- ◆ "Let me find that out for you."
- ◆ "I know someone who can help you with that."
- ◆ "Let me call the department that can help you."
- ◆ "I don't have that answer now, but I will call you back."

Think of an alternative to "next."

Some people have visions of a lamb going to slaughter when they hear "next." Other ways to let customers know that it is their turn include

- ◆ "May I help you?"
- ◆ "It's your turn."
- ◆ "My station's available."

Avoid negativity.

The following comments can cause conflict right away:

- ◆ "I don't know, and I don't care."
- ◆ "That's not my job."
- ◆ "Sorry, I can't."
- ◆ "You should have known better."
- ◆ "That's a stupid question."
- ◆ "Read the sign."
- ◆ "Let's get a move on."
- ◆ "I already told you that."
- ◆ "You'll have to do that yourself."

Watch Your Body Language

Your body language can give away what you are really feeling. It is often hard to be "up" all the time. People do experience "contact overload" when working with the public. If that happens to you, take a break. Go for a walk. Or, if you can't leave your area, make a conscious effort to change your mindset. Customers will pick up on your feelings and thoughts, especially if you are thinking any of the following. They are giveaways.

- I wish you would go.
- I don't like you.
- This job is boring.
- I could be at lunch if you would just get on with it.
- Can you speed it up?
- Can't you see I'm talking?

Use Positive Regard on the Phone

Working on the phone requires practicing the Law of Attraction too. If you envision customers needing your help, and you being able to give it, you will start out with positive regard. Positive regard means that you put the person you are talking with in a positive light. See Tool 5.2 for suggestions to keep phone conversations positive.

Work with Offensive Callers

If the customer is offensive or rude to the point of being insulting or discourteous to you, examples of responses you could use include:

- "I understand you are upset. I know we can work this out. If you respect me, and I respect you, we can solve this together. We need to listen to each other first."
- "If this is not a good time to talk, you can call me back. Maybe if we both think about solutions without becoming upset, it will be of more benefit. Call me back when we can problem solve together."
- "It would help me if . . . "
- "Time out! I want to hear what you are saying, but I have to ask you to slow down a bit."

If customers are not ready to converse in a civil way, and you have to call the person back or ask them to call you back, inform your boss. If you follow all the listening and problem-solving guidelines, it is rare that this will happen. Obviously, it is a last resort and may carry consequences. This one is up to you and your company to decide in terms of acceptability, but it deserves a discussion. Review Tool 5.2 for phone tips that will help you communicate positively with customers.

TOOL 5.2
A Dozen Musts for Phone Communication

1. Answer the phone with enthusiasm. Every customer deserves your best, every time.
2. Vary your tone and volume as you would in a conversation.
3. Take time to articulate.
4. Smile. Customers will feel it.
5. Listen as you would if the person were in front of you.
6. If you have to put someone on hold, ask the customer for permission to do that. Come back every 30 seconds to a minute with a progress report.
7. Greet the customer before you ask them if you can put them on hold.
8. If you transfer, make sure you transfer to the right person. Stay on the line until the transfer goes through to ensure the connection. Tell the customer where you are transferring to, and the phone number and name of the individual who will receive the call (if customers get disconnected, they will have an immediate reference to call back).
9. If the caller wants to speak with someone who is not available, offer to help.
10. Follow up with all requests and call the customer back if you have promised to do so.
11. Allow the customer to speak with a superior if necessary.
12. Close the call with a statement of appreciation.

STEP **5**

Keep Emails Short and to the Point

Think about the following when you write an email:

Approximate Number of Words

Gettysburg Address (Abraham Lincoln)	272
Bag of Lay's Potato Chips	401
IRS Form 1040EZ	418
Average *USA Today* cover story	1,200

Email Tips

1. Your employer owns your email and can view it at any time. In legal proceedings, it can be used in court.
2. Only send messages to "everyone" or "all employees" if you have authorization and permission.
3. WRITING IN CAPS AND IN RED IS THE EQUIVALENT OF SCREAMING.
4. Use an auto reply when you are away from the office.
5. Use question marks only for questions. Use only one question mark as you would in other written correspondence.
6. Send chain letters from home.
7. Use the subject line.
8. Put deadlines, meetings, and the most important information at the beginning of your email.
9. If you are angry, wait a day or two before sending out an email about the topic of your concern.
10. Use positive language.
11. Keep sentences between 14 and 20 words.
12. Use short paragraphs.
13. Bullet items for quick reference.
14. Respond to email within a day if possible or within four hours if you are answering an Internet request.

15. Respond only to the person who sent you an email, unless there is a reason to do otherwise.
16. Use "reply all" only when there is a reason to.
17. Email up the chain of command at your own risk.
18. Be kind.

For free tips on writing, visit www.basic-learning.com.

Positive thoughts go a long way, whether they are communicated in person or in writing. If you stay upbeat, you will be recognized for your ability and talent to turn situations around or make the workplace a better place. Ultimately, you should get more of what you want in terms of productive, worthwhile communications and relationships.

Complete Worksheets 5.2 and 5.3 to explore your positive qualities. Have fun and enjoy the results!

STEP **5**

WORKSHEET 5.2

Positive Qualities

Instructions: Write down all the positive qualities you have. Post the list where you can easily see it. Don't be embarrassed to look at it often. You can also do this as a team activity. You could also write a list of positive qualities that someone else has, and give the list to that person to post. You might start a trend!

WORKSHEET 5.3
The Power of a Positive Word

The following story is from an anonymous email.

A teacher asked her students to write down one positive thing about each person in her class. Names were clearly written on separate pieces of paper. When everyone wrote one nice thing on each person's paper, the papers were given to the owners whose names were on the top of the sheet.

Years later, these papers were found in the pockets of wounded war veterans and in places where you would never think something written years before would be found. Positive regard is powerful.

Do this activity with your team, your family, and your friends. You may discover positive aspects about yourself that you weren't aware of!

Put It All Together

Staying positive, even in challenging situations, is an important aspect of customer service. Step 6 delves further into staying positive and provides a step-by-step model and tools you can use for problem solving.

N O T E S

Aggressively Solve Problems—the Bigger the Better

OVERVIEW

- Investigate the root cause of problems
- Follow the model for problem solving
- Listen to complaints and show customer appreciation
- Use the Fantastic Service Equation

People who excel at their jobs solve problems. Nothing is more indicative of success in the workforce than solving problems. As Ron Willingham (2005) states in *Integrity Service*: "In a real sense, each of us controls our success level by the problems we choose to solve."

STEP **6**

Investigate the Root Cause of Problems

Problem solvers are highly respected. They usually move up the career ladder because of the value they bring to their organization. With information changing every nanosecond, learning and problem solving are critical. Nobody can know everything about his or her job. However, if you can find out where to access information and how to use it, you're a goldmine.

POINTER

"In a real sense, each of us controls our success level by the problems we choose to solve."

– *Ron Willingham,*

Integrity Service

People who get recognized at work deliver results. To reach desired outcomes, you have to investigate the issue or problem, look at reasons for the problem, discover ways to fix the problem, and act on your insights. Often, this process takes place naturally, without a definite structure. We learn how to solve problems early in life for survival and because of inborn curiosity. Infants are all over the place solving problems, often to their parents' dismay. On the other end of the spectrum, in business, top-level executives have the desire to solve problems and the curiosity to uncover creative solutions.

Although problem solving is, in part, second nature, solutions are not always well thought out. A famous company once ran a Superbowl ad about a special promotion (good thinking on the part of marketers), but neglected to tell the workforce about it. Thousands of calls the Monday after Sunday's game caught frontline staff by surprise. Instead of increasing sales, problems were created, not solved. There are countless stories like the Superbowl fiasco. You probably have some of your own.

Problems are caused by
◆ lack of information
◆ misinformation
◆ lack of communication
◆ faulty equipment
◆ failure to listen
◆ failure to follow through
◆ oversights
◆ change
◆ role confusion
◆ lack of teamwork
◆ underlying motivations
◆ technology.

Refer to Worksheet 6.1 to continue the "problems are caused by" list.

WORKSHEET 6.1

Identify Causes

Instructions: Work independently or with your team to finish the sentence: "Problems are caused by. . . "

_____

_____

_____

_____

_____

_____

_____

_____

_____

_____

_____

_____

_____

_____

The term *root cause* is equivalent to the "root of the problem." When professionals are looking at reasons for process failures or product malfunctions, they want to uncover the real source of the problem. When working with customers, root cause is also what you want to discover. If Mrs. Jones doesn't have any water, is it because she didn't pay her bill, or is she part of the neighborhood where a water pipe burst?

Define "Problem"

A problem occurs when there is gap between what is expected and what actually happened. For instance, if someone ordered a book, expected it to arrive on January 5, and that did not occur, there is a problem. If NASA expected a spacecraft to reach land by January 5 and it did not do so, there is a bigger problem involving more people and more resources. The root cause would have to be explored for both problems.

Follow the Model for Problem Solving

A model for solving problems helps avoid the "shoot from the hip" approach. It affords you a systematic way of investigating and solving a problem. The following model has the elements necessary to accomplish your goals.

1. **Describe the problem.**

    Express the problem by clearly describing it. This could be to the customer, to your boss, to your employee, or to a co-worker. Describe the gap between what exists and what you want. Review the following example of a problem at a doctor's office.

    What exists: "We have a referral, but that doctor is not available."

    What you want: "We need to find another doctor."

2. Research and Clarify the Issues.

Determine the reasons for the problem. Research what needs to be done to correct the gap. Redefine the problem if necessary.

Research: "In addition, it looks like that doctor is not on your plan anymore."

3. Offer an Outcome.

After researching and clarifying the issues, an outcome should emerge as being viable. Or, the outcome may require further exploration.

Outcome: "I found a doctor on your plan who can take you tomorrow! I heard he was nice as well!"

4. Imagine Other Possibilities.

You have solved the problem this time; however, the next phase of problem solving involves thinking about what can be done if the problem arises in the future, or imagining new systems or techniques for problem resolution. For instance, it might be great to have a personal computer available that patients can use to find the names of doctors and the insurance plans they accept. Giving a patient the name of a back-up doctor would also help in case he or she needs help for a similar problem in the future.

5. Plan for Success.

Planning may be for improvements or to ensure that the current solution is accomplished. In this scenario, giving the patient directions to the physician's office would be a way of planning to ensure that the outcome is achieved. It is also providing additional information. Providing additional information and ways to prevent problems are two of the most important ways to gain customer loyalty.

Use Worksheet 6.2 to practice solving a problem you would like to address.

WORKSHEET 6.2

Solve the Problem

Instructions: Identify a job-related problem. Work individually or with your team to solve the problem using the model presented in Step 6.

Listen to Complaints

Jane Barlow and Claus Moller (2008) wrote *A Complaint Is a Gift: Recovering Customer Loyalty When Things Go Wrong.* The title expresses what the authors hoped to convey: When customers complain, they are giving you a gift—their feedback. They are also giving you the opportunity to fix a problem. If you can frame a complaint in that manner, and you know how to solve problems, you have many opportunities to show your expertise. Listen to complaints and solve as many problems as you can—the bigger the better. You will reap the rewards in customer appreciation and in your own career growth.

Customer Appreciation

The following commentary is from an appreciative customer. When she spoke about what occurred in the story, she was aware that many customer service providers would help in the same way; however, she was also aware that some would not, and that "procedures" would get in the way of service. See how one gesture captured the loyalty of a customer.

The speaker feature in my cell phone died a few days before I was going to a conference where I needed speaker access. I went to the T-Mobile store where I purchased the phone and asked if they could exchange it for me. The agent said she was unable to make the exchange, but she called the company and asked if it could send me a new phone. We were heading into a holiday weekend. Monday was a holiday and I was leaving town on Wednesday. The agent stressed that I needed to receive the phone by Tuesday and asked the representative to waive the shipping fee, which the staff member agreed to do. I thanked the agent and asked her if she could give me the phone number of her supervisor. I wanted to relay how helpful she had been. I reached the supervisor, who agreed she was indeed a wonderful employee. I asked if the agent could get special recognition for her service. I was told that, in fact, there was going to be a banquet in which one exemplary employee would be awarded a trip for two to Hawaii. I later found out that the agent who has been so helpful to me was awarded the trip. I was thrilled and impressed with T-Mobile's follow through.

Take Action to Give Customers Satisfaction

The poem below was written by my dad, who owned Flair of Miami, a dress manufacturing firm that had the longest tenure in the city of Miami, Florida. For more than 40 years, he provided outstanding customer service based on his belief in "doing the right thing."

Complaints

Hundreds of people and many more
All have complaints and they are by the score.
Their bills don't add up exactly right
Their clothing purchase is far too tight.
Eight hours a day you hear these complaints
You need, no question, the patience of saints.
But the job you hold is one you requested
And every day it's your patience that's tested.
You must take whatever action
To give the client satisfaction;
Your employer expects this, that is true
But more importantly, so should you.
— *Jack Kamin, age 90*

Use the Fantastic Service Equation

In order to have a satisfied customer, you need to start off on the right foot, anticipate needs, solve problems, and appreciate the customer. Following these steps will give you the tools you need to please customers and experience positive relationships. The "Fantastic Service Equation" in Tool 6.1 can be used to remind yourself of what you have learned and help you follow the steps for excellent service.

POINTER Two of the Fantastic Service Equation components, "Checking Results" and "Leaving the Door Open," are designed to prevent problems from occurring and to reassure the customer that you have a proactive mindset.

Two of the Fantastic Service Equation components, "Checking Results" and "Leaving the Door Open," are designed to prevent problems from occurring and to reassure the customer that you have a proactive mindset.

TOOL 6.1

The Fantastic Service Equation: How to deliver fantastic service every time

Equation Components

Greeting the Customer

Responsive service starts with a responsive greeting. You only get one first chance to impress a customer, and that first chance lasts only a matter of seconds.

Customers expect a friendly greeting, complete with eye contact, a smile, and receptive body language. It's basic. It is recognizing a person's worth right off the bat. A greeting establishes rapport. It immediately says, "I'm here to serve," which is what service is all about.

Greetings come in all forms. It's the parking lot attendant, who says, "Glad to see you today!" It's the security guard who opens the door for you in the morning, walks you to the elevator, and pushes the button of your floor for you. It's the librarian who says "hello" and smiles before you do. It's the customer service representative who answers the phone with a smile and means it when she says, "How can I help you today?"

Determining Needs

Finding out what a customer really needs determines the rest of the interaction. Listening and asking questions are fundamental to this part of the equation. When you listen, you are giving the customer your undivided attention and respect. Listening can help with sales, customer concerns, and problem solving. Proactive listening is the key ingredient in providing responsive, empathetic service.

Listening involves your total concentration, the ability to paraphrase, to understand thoughts and feelings, and to work together with the customer for the customer and the company's benefit.

continued on next page

Meeting Needs

Once needs are determined, it's time to act. Responding entails being reliable and assuring. It's acting quickly, with confidence, and figuring out what you can do to make that customer happy. It is giving the customer what was promised, finding out information, delivering a product or service on time, having someone available to answer a question or answer the phone, and guiding the customer toward a solution.

Making the Moment Memorable

Here's where your creativity comes into play. This is where you do something special. It could be something big. It could be something little. Whatever it is, it makes the customer feel good. A memorable moment could be as simple as walking someone to his destination rather than pointing or telling him where to go. It could be staying after hours to complete a transaction. It could be calling a customer to see if the solution you agreed on worked. It could be a sales rep coming to check the installation of equipment she sold. It's the "wow" factor—the surprise of an unexpected act of kindness.

Nordstrom, is a department store that is well known for outstanding service, once had a disgruntled customer come in with a defective tire. The store gladly took the tire back and refunded the customer's money.

What's so unusual about this story? Nordstrom doesn't sell tires.

Checking Results

This is an easy and on-going way to see if you are giving fantastic service: *Just ask.*

Companies and organizations spend a lot of money on surveys, comment cards, and other types of data to get customer feedback. But, you can be the first to get feedback, just by asking. Even the simplest question, "Is there anything else we can do for you?" said with sincerity is a way to see if all the customer's needs have been met. Or, "How was our service today?"

You can also promote other services when you check results. If you see that you can offer an option of another service, or you can tell customers

Tool 6.1, continued

something they didn't know about your organization that can help them in the future, you have helped to solidify that relationship and your organization's image in the customer's eyes.

Responses might not always be positive. Customers may complain. A complaint, however, is just an opportunity. As discussed earlier in this step, a complaint points you toward ways to make things better or to improve. Handling a complaint can be a memorable moment.

> A complaint is a memorable moment waiting to happen.

So, involve customers in your organization. Ask them their opinion. Pave the wave for customer loyalty.

Leaving the Door Open

There are many ways to encourage customers to do more business or to feel comfortable coming back to your organization. Customers like to be appreciated. It is a way to recognize them and support their patronage. Leaving the door open is a way to say, "Please come back" or "Thanks for your support." You might say: "Thanks for being our guest here," or "Hope you come back to buy your next birthday present," or "Call me personally if you have any more questions," or "I'll be looking forward to seeing you when you come back with the information we talked about."

(Used with permission, Maxine Kamin, *Customer Service Training*, American Society for Training & Development, 2006)

Review Tool 6.2 to reinforce your service expertise. Use Tool 6.3 for suggestions on how your organization can ensure customers are receiving excellent service.

TOOL 6.2

FSET Survey–Fantastic Service Every Time

Instructions: Put the number you choose in the space provided.

1 = Almost Always   2 = Most of the Time   3 = Sometimes   4 = Rarely

GREETING

I say hello to everyone when I come into work—those in my work unit and those I see on the way in.	
When working with customers, I make eye contact first and greet them with a smile.	
I answer the phone with a smile.	
When people are waiting, I acknowledge them and let them know I will be with them as soon as I can.	
TOTAL	

DETERMINING NEEDS

I find it easy to listen to customers, even when they are rambling.	
I repeat or paraphrase important requests to ensure that I understand what a customer needs.	
I am good at dealing with intense emotions at work.	
Even if I think I know what customers want, I ask questions that help me figure out what customers really need.	
TOTAL	

MEETING NEEDS

If a customer is angry with me, or has "an attitude," I go out of my way to give that person good service.	
I apologize for errors, whether or not I was responsible for the error.	
I do things quickly.	
I keep my word.	
TOTAL	

STEP **6**

Instructions: Put the number you choose in the space provided.

1 = Almost Always   2 = Most of the Time   3 = Sometimes   4 = Rarely

MAKING THE MOMENT MEMORABLE

I would take time out of my schedule to walk a person where he or she needs to go, rather than just give directions.	
If a customer has called several times, I will make a call myself to ensure that the customer reaches the right person.	
I welcome the chance to help other workers solve problems for customers, even when I'm busy.	
I enjoy finding ways to please customers.	
TOTAL	

CHECKING RESULTS

I ask customers what they think about our service.	
I ask if there is anything else we can do, even if the transaction is finished.	
I ask customers if they will come back, or if they would use our services again.	
I ask customers for their opinions on how we can make our service even better.	
TOTAL	

LEAVING THE DOOR OPEN

I give my name or card to customers in case they need to contact me again.	
I sometimes follow up by calling a customer to see if a problem or issue was resolved.	
I invite customers to come back if I think they might be interested in something we have to offer.	
I appreciate customers for coming in and using our services.	
TOTAL	

STEP 6

continued on next page

Tool 6.2, continued

FSET Survey

Review each category to see if there are improvements that you want to make. Are there any questions where "almost always" or "most of the time" may not be enough?

For each category, list ways you can continue to demonstrate excellent customer service skills and ways you can improve.

Greeting

Continue	
Improve	

Determining Needs

Continue	
Improve	

Meeting Needs

Continue	
Improve	

Making the Moment Memorable

Continue	
Improve	

Checking Results

Continue	
Improve	

Leaving the Door Open

Continue	
Improve	

(Used with permission, Maxine Kamin, *Customer Service Training*, American Society for Training & Development, 2006)

TOOL 6.3

Ways for Your Organization to Check Results

Instructions: In addition to checking results personally, your company may use other ways to ensure that customers are receiving fantastic service, including:

Checking Results	How This Works
One-on-one interviews	May be done on a formal or informal basis; provides data to identify trends and common concerns.
Researching records	Data that already exists, such as hourly, daily, and monthly sales; comparison of previous years and market share (just some ways to determine customer preferences). This is also a way to prevent problems that might occur such as being out of stock because of lack of information or trend analysis.
Questionnaires or surveys	Conducted to determine characteristics of customers and their likes and dislikes. Surveys also are used to identify provider service, as well as areas that need improvement. If certain areas emerge as less than adequate, training or coaching may be part of the solution.
Observation	Done at work every day, observation can be even more of a useful data gathering tool when you decide ahead of time what you want to observe. Customer observation is invaluable. Staff observation is useful and can provide ways for the whole company to use the Fantastic Service Equation and observe each other's success.

Put It All Together

Step 6 presented the Model for Problem Solving, a step-by-step approach that will help you define the real issues and develop solutions. Using the "Fantastic Service Equation" tool ensures excellent service in all parts of the customer transaction. Step 7 conveys the importance of an apology, and the necessity to fix the problem as soon as possible to recover from mistakes gracefully.

STEP

6

Recover from Mistakes Gracefully

Apologize

Fix the problem

Offer something of value

Follow up

Recovery is making good on a mistake. No matter how hard you try, you, or the company you work for, can make an error. Think of a mistake as an opportunity to regain the customer's loyalty. As you read in Step 2, customers who have a problem that gets resolved are actually more loyal than those who never had a problem at all.

The following are ways you can increase the probability that a customer will be forgiving.

Apologize

When you apologize, you are recognizing that a customer is dissatisfied. You are not necessarily apologizing for something you did, or even something that the company did. Maybe the customer had to walk a long way from the parking lot and wants you to know how long it took him to get there. You could say, "That was a long way for you to walk," or "I'm sorry that you had to spend time walking that you didn't anticipate." It's not your fault that the customer had to walk so far. The apology is simply to acknowledge the customer's inconvenience.

However, if an error was made, an apology is essential. Equally important is determining who is responsible for what went wrong; for example, not having an item ready when promised or a product that doesn't function properly. In those cases, an apology is in order. If the customer is upset about something that you're not sure was the organization's fault or if the concern is about a product dysfunction, you need to apologize for whatever the client had to endure. An apology is an expected part of customer service; it is not an extra. It is a common courtesy.

Fix the Problem

We have talked about problem-solving techniques, questions, and ways to stay positive in situations where you have to make good on a promise. The promise is the company or organization's guarantee to deliver. Whatever promise was broken, or perceived to be broken, you need to fix it.

Whatever the customer thinks is a problem is one. Is the customer always right? No. However, the customer is always right in his or her mind. It's not up to us to be the judge and jury. It's not up to us to save the store: "Aha, I caught you. You broke that yourself." It's not up to us to question someone's decision to return something or to register a complaint. Fix the problem as quickly and efficiently as possible. Exchange the merchandise. Give a credit. Avoid arguing at all costs because, in extreme cases, it will cost—possibly one person's business for life, and word of mouth tales that might reach millions of people costing an untold amount of lost revenue.

Offer Something of Value

Although you may not be able to make a "peace offering" yourself, a token of good will is one way to soothe a person who is annoyed. This is not a ploy. It is a way to make someone feel better. Remember the goal is to make the customer feel good.

Customers have come to expect that something extra will be offered to them if they have been loyal to the organization. If you read posts on consumer websites, you will see comments from customers who want retribution with a gift certificate, movie pass, complimentary dinner, new computer, or refunds of expenses. Some consumers even want retribution when the mistake was theirs.

The following story is an example of shoppers who were incensed that a store did not offer compensation for their trouble. It also demonstrates how an exception could have saved a family a lot of discomfort. The drama and pain that companies can save customers goes far beyond dollars and cents.

Christina and her mom, Elaine, were shopping for a bed, which would be the first big purchase that Christina was buying with her own money.

The mother-daughter team saw a box spring and mattress they both liked. Elaine asked the salesperson if she had a headboard that would fit the box spring and mattress. The salesperson enthusiastically showed them a headboard that Christina loved.

Elaine wanted to be sure that the headboard would connect to the frame without any additional preparation or special equipment. She had nobody to assemble the bed. The salesperson responded by saying, "Sure! No problem! This headboard will attach easily."

The next day, Sunday, all the items were delivered at 7:30 a.m. Although the drivers woke them up, Elaine and Christina were excited to get the new furniture. However, as soon as the deliverymen began assembling the bed, they discovered that they couldn't attach the headboard to the frame because the assembly would require special bolts and supports. Mom and daughter were devastated.

Christina called the salesperson who sold her the bed. The salesperson said, "Oh, yeah, that's happened before. You can go to the hardware store and purchase carriage bolts and have somebody attach it." Clearly upset, Christina said, "I paid for delivery and set up! I don't have anyone to help us with this, and if we do it our-selves, we might ruin the headboard."

The deliverymen heard the conversation and were very under-standing. They told Elaine and Christina that it might be best to go back to the store, and that it opened at 9:00.

Mother and daughter arrived at the store at 9:00 only to find that it didn't open until 11:00. To kill time, they went out to breakfast.

When the store opened, they spoke with their original salesper-son. She showed them headboards that "might work better." Even though Christina could not understand why the salesperson didn't show her "headboards that might work better" to begin with, she looked at the alternatives. She didn't like any of them. She said that she would just return the headboard she had and she didn't want another.

Then the salesperson recommended that Christina keep the headboard, but get a footboard from another set from the same manufacturer. Christina was frustrated, pointing out that the two sets didn't match, not to mention the fact that they couldn't assemble the headboard, which was why they were in the store in the first place. However, she was now warming up to the idea of having a footboard.

Christina found a headboard and a footboard that she liked. She asked if she could get the items for the price of a twin set rather than a standard. She explained that this would be within her budget, and expressed to the salesperson that she and her mom had gone through a lot of unnecessary trouble. The salesperson refused Christina's request because she couldn't key the correct numbers into the computer. Elaine figured that someone could determine how to make this exception and revise a standard price on the company's computer. She asked to see a manager. In a very stern tone, the salesperson said, "We do not negotiate here. The prices are what they are." Elaine was not able to get any further.

They left the store. Christina was upset, but Elaine said, "If this is the worst thing that happens to us in life, we're lucky. It's material stuff." Christina was still upset.

On Monday, Christina's boyfriend, Eric, came over and saw that she was still livid. He decided to take it upon himself to go to the furniture store. He saw the same salesperson, explained the story, and the salesperson said, "Oh, yes, I remember your girlfriend. I just happen to have a package of plates that might help. You put them between the bed and frame before it is bolted."

Eric took the plates and went to Home Depot, where he purchased carriage bolts. When he got back to Christina's house, Christina wasn't happy. She didn't want Eric to work on the headboard. She wanted to return it and buy a matching headboard and footboard from a different store.

Christina went to work feeling very stressed. Eric was mad because Christina wouldn't let him fix the headboard. He wanted to help.

When the deliverymen came to pick up the headboard, Christina said, "This is the headboard from hell." Hearing only a synopsis of the story from Christina, they nodded and said, "This isn't the first time this has happened."

A month later, Christina got a bill for an "exchange fee" for the merchandise. She received no consideration from the store when she explained that she did not exchange the headboard; she returned it because it could not be assembled in the way she was promised.

At the time of this writing, mother and daughter are still contesting the $60 fee.

How many "touch points"—or times the store could have pleased the customer—were ignored in this scenario? The last resort in this case is recovery since, from the beginning, the salesperson should have known about installation procedures or been truthful; we don't know which. At the very least, the salesperson would have recovered by selling the merchandise for the price of a twin set rather than a standard, and some of the continued annoyance, family conflict, and distress might have been mitigated. People want to be compensated for what they consider to be unfair inconvenience. They want you to make good.

Give Coupons and Advance Sales Notices

Another way to show understanding of the customer's inconvenience is to offer coupons, advance sales notices, information the customer might not have known about, or other bonuses.

Follow Up

A follow-up call is usually over and above what customers expect. When your consideration goes beyond the moment, it is appreciated, sometimes with surprise, but always with appreciation.

In contrast to Elaine and Christina's story, here's a recovery story sent to me by a friend.

My daughter wanted a particular poster for her college dorm. Walmart usually carries the poster but it was out of stock on the day we went to get it. A salesperson in the department said she would call the vendor and let us know when the poster was going to be back in stock. A few weeks later, true to her word, the salesperson called to say that the poster came in, and asked if we wanted her to hold it for us. Today, even high-end stores don't go to that length for a customer! The next day, I called the salesperson's supervisor to relay the story. I was assured that the salesperson would be verbally recognized at a team meeting, and that a letter of commendation would be put in her file.

Refer to Worksheet 7.1 for team discussion topics that will allow you to address issues of empowerment, teamwork, and customer satisfaction.

WORKSHEET 7.1

Resolving Conflicts

Instructions: Brainstorm these ideas without evaluating the suggestions that are made. List the ideas on a flipchart or take notes to distribute after the meeting.

What are some of our common customer conflicts? _____

_____

_____

_____

_____

How have we resolved the conflicts in the past? _____

_____

_____

_____

_____

Are there better ways to resolve any of the situations? What are they? _____

_____

_____

_____

_____

What are exceptions that each level staff member in our team can authorize?

_____

_____

_____

_____

What is the best process for escalating issues? _____

_____

_____

_____

What is the best way to communicate the results of a conflict? _____

_____

_____

_____

The Role of the Leader

If you are a manager or a leader in your organization, you can help your staff members by offering assistance in situations where customers expect more than they are getting, or more than what your staff can authorize. If you are able to approve an exception, the customer will appreciate the gesture. Not only will it foster goodwill, you will increase the chances for repeat business with the customer.

Work with your staff members for resolution of customers' concerns. At times, managers make decisions without explaining their reasons to their staff. Sometimes they please the customer and displease the employee. You can avoid these circumstances by discussing your role with your team in staff meetings, and by deciding together how to best handle common situations. Of course, there will be times when you have to deal with situations that are not predictable. Judgment calls are a part of your responsibility as a leader.

Although taking responsibility is essential, motivating your staff is equally as important, and solving problems together can be motivating. Making decisions without explanations or follow-up with the staff member involved in the initial conflict can cause resentment. Be proactive and work with your staff. Explain that you are not *overruling* your team members when you approve an exception; you are making a decision to waive the rules based on the factors that you see. Let them know that you appreciate them when they try to stay within your rules and bring possible exceptions to your attention. Discuss the best way to communicate in difficult situations, and what you can empower them to do themselves. These types of discussions build trust among the whole team.

♦ ♦ ♦

Put It All Together

Mistakes do happen. When they do, it is critical in customer service to apologize, fix the problem, and offer something of value to recover gracefully and retain customer loyalty. Understanding customer differences is also an important key to providing excellent service. Step 8 describes different personality types and learning styles, and gives you ways to respond to a variety of customer behaviors.

STEP **7**

STEP
7

Give Customers and Yourself a Break

Personality types

Respond as a customer

Intelligence types and
learning styles

Carl Jung (1875–1961), Swiss
psychiatrist and researcher, be-
lieved that people are born with
characteristics and preferences
that form their personality. His
discoveries about human nature
peaked the interest of Katherine
Cook Briggs (1875–1968) and her
daughter, Isabel Briggs Myers (1897–1980). They conducted their
own research and created the Myers-Briggs Type Indicator (MBTI)
to assess personality traits based on Jung's research.

The MBTI is the world's most widely used instrument for understanding normal personality differences. It allows people who take
the self-scoring instrument to determine their preferences based on
the traits in Tool 8.1.

Knowing that people are born with different ways of looking at things and different approaches to making decisions can be
comforting. If you have ever wondered why people aren't like you,
why they are not more rational, more compassionate, more understanding, more organized, or less rigid, it may be because of inborn
traits. They may need help in seeing things your way because it

is not natural for them to comprehend information or feelings the same way you do. Conversely, you may need help seeing their perspective and point of view.

When you work with customers and colleagues, your personalities and their personalities impact interactions.

TOOL 8.1
Preferences—An Overview

How you get your energy	Extraversion (from others and the outer world) or Introversion (from internal reflection)
How you take in information	Sensing (facts, figures, and observations that are real and tangible) or Intuition (patterns, intuition, and the big picture)
How you make decisions	Thinking (by logic and objectivity) or Feeling (by what is personally important to you and to others involved)
How you orient yourself to the external world	Judging (planned and orderly) or Perceiving (flexible, spontaneous, wanting to experience and understand life rather than control it)

Personality Types

Extraversion and Introversion

Extraverts are expressive. They are at ease when talking, and they enjoy socializing. As customers, they will talk about their experiences, sometimes in great detail. If you are an extravert, it may be challenging to listen because, just like the customers you are serving, it is likely that you want to talk and explain yourself. It's common for extraverts to think out loud. If both you and the customer are trying to think out loud, nobody is listening.

POINTER

When you work with customers and colleagues, your personalities and their personalities impact interactions.

Extraverts get their batteries charged and their energy revitalized by conversing. As staff members, they need frequent social breaks. Extraverts get things done, and they like variety. They speak up at meetings. Sometimes, in their enthusiasm to be expressive, they don't think before they speak, and may end up revealing more than they had intended.

Introverts get their energy from quiet reflection. They speak when they have something important to say. Otherwise, they are content to listen. They prefer to interact one on one, or in small groups, and can experience contact overload when they are in crowds for long periods of time or when interacting nonstop. Introverts need their quiet time to regroup. Taking a walk or a break may suffice to recharge their batteries.

Introverts need extraverts to bring them out, ask questions, and elicit opinions. Extraverts need introverts to listen, reflect, and focus in depth on issues.

Sensing and Intuition

People who prefer sensing are realists. They take in information by what they can see, hear, touch, and smell. They ascribe to "only the facts, ma'am, only the facts," a popular saying on the TV classic *Dragnet*. Sensors are good at figuring out concrete things.

People who prefer intuition are the visionaries who like change and enjoy figuring out new ways to do things. Whereas sensors might say, "If it ain't broke, don't fix it," intuitors might say, "There must be a way to make things better." For customers and staff members who prefer sensing, it is critical to go step by step in explanations. For those who prefer intuition, alternatives and choices are often appreciated.

A good team has a mixture of personality types, including those who prefer intuition to provide the vision of the organization, and those who prefer sensing to make it happen.

STEP **8**

Thinking and Feeling

Thinkers make their decision by logic. They are analytical and seek objectivity. They are sometimes perceived as critical since their natural way of making decisions is to evaluate and provide alternatives or objectivity. Feelers take into account what the entire group is feeling, and they make decisions based on their values—on what they think is right or moral. As colleagues, feelers like to be appreciated for their insights about people. They also enjoy appreciating others. As customers, feelers are sensitive to nonverbal cues, and they expect you to be compassionate. Thinkers might be more interested in the logic of your explanations and the effectiveness of your service.

Judging and Perceiving

Those who prefer to use their judging process like to plan, organize, make decisions, and come to closure. As customers, they might be impatient with considering alternatives, and frustrated when they must wait for decisions. They want things done and settled so they can move on. Those who prefer to use their perceiving process feel constrained by detailed plans and final decisions. They want to stay open to new information and to adapt to the moment. In making buying decisions, they would be less likely to make a decision on the spot.

Everybody uses all preferences at one time or another. What you prefer is just that—what comes most naturally to you, like writing with your right hand instead of your left if you are right-handed. Try writing with the hand you do not usually use. That will give you an idea of the comfort level you have with the preference that is opposite to your natural one.

Worksheet 8.1 gives you a list of possible customer behaviors, based on personality type. Follow the directions to see how you might behave as a customer and to gain insight as to how others might function.

WORKSHEET 8.1

Different Customer Personalities

Instructions: The following are behaviors that might be exhibited by different customer types. Which behaviors do you most identify with as a customer? Circle the bulleted customer behaviors that might apply to you. Add the circles up in each category.

Extraverts (E)—Possible Behaviors	Introverts (I)—Possible Behaviors
◆ Talk freely about what they are thinking	◆ May tell you part of the story and check to see if you are listening
◆ May repeat themselves	◆ May quietly wait to ask if you can help
◆ Get off topic	
◆ Talk about their personal experiences	◆ Want to think through what they need to say before they communicate
◆ May tell you more than you want to know	◆ Want to develop rapport
◆ Like to be sociable	◆ May respond slowly because they are thinking
◆ Are expressive	◆ Would not like to "make a scene"
◆ May talk quickly	
◆ Want feedback	◆ May not want to bother you
Square 1: Number of items circled ____	Square 2: Number of items circled ____

Sensors (S)—Possible Behaviors	Intuitors (N)—Possible Behaviors
◆ Want facts and figures	◆ Like to see the big picture
◆ Need to see things in black and white	◆ Are good at imagining possibilities
◆ Take direction well	◆ Are creative
◆ Are good at details	◆ Are interested in the future
◆ May not see the whole picture	◆ Do not like routine or lots of details
◆ Need solid evidence	
◆ Want to know that you have a well thought out plan	◆ Like to change things for the better
◆ Are suspect of change	◆ Can jump in anywhere; don't go in order
Square 3: Number of items circled ____	Square 4: Number of items circled ____

STEP 8

continued on next page

Thinkers (T)—Possible Behaviors	Feelers (F)—Possible Behaviors
◆ Are logical and usually think that they are right	◆ Want to establish rapport
◆ May tell you what to do	◆ Want to create solutions that are mutually agreeable
◆ May be impatient	◆ Have definite values
◆ Want immediate attention	◆ Are concerned about how decisions affect people
◆ Don't want to wait	◆ Want harmony instead of discord
◆ May give the impression that they don't think you're capable	◆ May get their feelings hurt or get angry if you are abrupt
◆ Expect you to fix problems	◆ Get upset if they or others are treated disrespectfully
◆ Want brief and concise answers	◆ Want everyone to get along
◆ May assume that you should know what they want	◆ May not want people to "get in trouble" because of a mistake
◆ Can act annoyed	
◆ May try to create a win–lose situation	
Square 5: Number of items circled ____	Square 6: Number of items circled ____

Judgers (J)—Possible Behaviors	Perveivers (P)—Possible Behaviors
◆ Need to know timelines	◆ Go with the flow
◆ Want to know when decisions will be made	◆ Are flexible
◆ Follow-up on your verbal deadlines	◆ May need to be reminded of deadlines and priorities
◆ Keep things in neat order	◆ Like to start things more than they like to finish them
◆ Are not comfortable with "things left hanging"	◆ Have piles of things all around; don't put a lot of value on being neat
◆ Need to have a well thought out plan	◆ Are spontaneous
◆ Don't like surprises	◆ May take a while to make a decision
◆ Need to be prepared for changes	◆ May change their mind
Square 7: Number of items circled ____	Square 8: Number of items circled ____

STEP
8

- ◆ The left and right squares indicate different types of preferences. Determine which squares have the highest numbers, 1 or 2, 3 or 4, 5 or 6, 7 or 8.

- ◆ List the four preferred areas you chose, using the letters that are in parentheses for quadrant titles; for example, INFP _____ .

- ◆ If you look at all the behaviors you chose in the quadrants, do they describe you as a customer?

- ◆ If you tied in any areas, pick which quadrants you think are most like you.

If some of the behaviors in Worksheet 8.1 described you, Tool 8.2 will give you ideas about responding to people who have similar preferences, as well as those who have different preferences. There are no rights and wrongs in personality types. All have gifts to offer and to receive.

To take a quiz on your personality type, visit www.kiersey.com.

TOOL 8.2

Responding to Customer Types

Extraverts

Your response:

- ◆ Listen

- ◆ Paraphrase

- ◆ Ask open-ended questions to build rapport and closed-ended questions to focus the discussion

- ◆ Be congenial

- ◆ Don't expect to come to conclusions right away

- ◆ Suggest alternatives

continued on next page

STEP **8**

Introverts

Your response:

- ◆ Greet with enthusiasm
- ◆ Ask open-ended questions
- ◆ Encourage communication
- ◆ Allow time for responses
- ◆ Don't interrupt
- ◆ Be comfortable with silence

Sensors

Your response:

- ◆ Give facts and details
- ◆ Be practical and realistic
- ◆ Show how things are similar to what they already know
- ◆ Be clear and direct
- ◆ Explain step by step what you are going to do

Intuitors

Your response:

- ◆ Give the overall picture first
- ◆ Allow time for discussion
- ◆ Validate their vision
- ◆ Ask for their cooperation in filling out required paperwork
- ◆ Repeat details you need to get across
- ◆ Don't get frustrated
- ◆ Walk them through it

Thinkers

Your response:

- ◆ Listen intently and follow the listening guidelines
- ◆ Use "I" statements ("I can help you")
- ◆ Get things done quickly and accurately
- ◆ Try and reach a decision that they perceive as their own
- ◆ Keep the person informed about what you can do
- ◆ Offer alternatives, if appropriate
- ◆ Be businesslike

STEP **8**

- Show you care
- Be confident that you can help
- Create a win–win situation
- Show that you are capable by your skillful actions

Feelers
Your response:

- Be sincere and empathetic
- Show interest in what they are saying
- Listen to concerns
- Paraphrase
- Be personable and friendly
- Show that you care about their concerns
- Make sure your body language is receptive
- Appreciate their suggestions
- Validate their feelings
- Involve them in decisions

Judgers
Your response:

- Have things in order
- Make sure your deadlines are accurate
- Follow up on commitments
- Have a plan and follow it
- Be clear about expectations

Perceivers
Your response:

- Try to be flexible
- Don't get upset with lack of order
- Help prioritize
- Be clear about important deadlines
- Allow flexibility when you can
- Help in planning
- Follow up with reminders

Respond as a Customer

In Worksheet 8.1, you reviewed how you might respond as a customer. Consider the following recommendations by Dr. Brad Stocker, professor at Miami-Dade College, to increase the probability that you will receive good service when you are the customer.

1. To facilitate satisfaction, be sure that you are doing business with the company who made the transaction. This can be confirmed with receipts or other paper verification. If receipts are not available, other forms of recordkeeping, such as electronic records, email transactions, or credit card bills, can help identify the business. If the product was a gift, you may have to rely on the goodwill of the company to accept your word with no proof of purchase.

2. Be clear about what can realistically be expected to resolve the problem. For example, if the item in question was a gift for which you have no receipt, it is unlikely that you will get cash back for the gift. You may get store credit, but with no receipt, you will probably be offered the lowest sale price for the item. If the gift is broken or malfunctions, the store may redirect you to the manufacturer.

3. When you contact the company, verify that you have the right person in that company to resolve the problem. State the problem and listen to the other person restate it so that you are both clear about the issue. Offer the outcome that would satisfy you and listen to the company representative's description of possible solutions.

4. Be open and flexible. You might be offered a resolution that is not what you had decided on in number 2. Consider what the company representative says. If you are still not satisfied at this point, express your concerns clearly, politely, and firmly.

5. Listen for indications that the representative is actually trying to help you. Recognizing and acknowledging that the person is making an attempt to help is an act of kindness. When the customer representative says, "Let me

see what I can do," take a moment to say, "Thank you, I really appreciate your help." Small courtesies go a long way to smooth the path to a positive outcome, and they make other people feel good.

Frontline service providers have great responsibility to help resolve your problem, but very limited authority. At some point, your situation may exceed that authority. When this impasse is apparent, you might want to ask for a supervisor. Service providers are often given the implicit, if not explicit, instructions to resolve the problem quickly and not to involve a supervisor unless the customer requests it. In most cases, when you request a supervisor, you will get one, although it might take some time.

Another reason to request a supervisor is if the customer representative appears to be unwilling to look for a reasonable resolution.

6. Make a human-to-human connection whenever possible. While your problem is the issue, the people who are helping you have lives and struggles. It may be that the voice at the other end of the phone is coming from someone who is in pain, has a cold, lost a family member, or is in some other kind of stress. They can be touched by a caring gesture more than you might expect.

7. Understand that the person with whom you are speaking is not the company. They are company representatives, not the board of directors. This does not excuse any behavior less than helpful. However, be careful not to take out your frustrations, your urgency, your pressures, or your other life stresses on the representative.

If the representative was helpful and courteous, it would be a nice gesture to let the supervisor know. It would also be good to let the representative know that you appreciate his or her help and that you will be passing the compliment on to the supervisor. It is equally your right and perhaps your responsibility to let the supervisor know if the representative was discourteous or unwilling to help or listen.

8. Know when to quit. The only point that is more difficult than being flexible is knowing when to quit. You need to keep your ego out of the way of your behavior and decision making. Be clear about the importance of your goal of satisfaction. One definition of satisfaction could and should be: I tried. Assess whether further pursuit of the initial outcome is worth the time and other expenses that you will need to invest. Consider the goal. Not all goals are equal in importance. For example, trying to return a gift for which you have no receipt is nowhere near the goal of getting the correct medicine.

Hanging on to a fight that you may or may not win, simply because you need to win, may cost you more in terms of psychic health, increase your anger, raise your stress, and/or debilitate your well being much more than the potential benefit of winning the battle with the representative. More often than not, representatives will leave your encounter wishing they could have helped you. In the end, it is really better that all involved come away satisfied and respected.

Types of Intelligence and Learning Styles

In 1983, Dr. Howard Gardner, professor of education at Harvard University, introduced his theory of multiple intelligences. The theory suggests that the traditional notion of intelligence, based on I.Q. testing, is too limited. Instead, Dr. Gardner proposed eight different intelligences to account for a broader range of human potential. These include:

- **Linguistic intelligence** (word smart)
- **Logical-mathematical intelligence** (number/reasoning smart)
- **Spatial intelligence** (picture smart)
- **Bodily-kinesthetic intelligence** (body smart)
- **Musical intelligence** (music smart)

STEP 8

- ◆ **Interpersonal intelligence** (people smart)
- ◆ **Intrapersonal intelligence** (self smart)
- ◆ **Naturalist intelligence** (nature smart)

WORKSHEET 8.2

Smart Intelligence

Instructions: This worksheet is for you to get an idea of the eight intelligences as they apply to you. Check the items that describe you. You will have some in different categories, or possibly all, since we all have multiple intelligences.

For a full discussion of multiple intelligences, refer to Howard Gardner's (1983) *Frames of Mind*.

Linguistic Intelligence

1.___I was very talkative at an early age.

2.___I love to curl up with a good book.

3.___I like poetry and stories.

4.___I have an easy time memorizing information, scripts, or poems.

5.___Sometimes people don't understand what I am saying.

6.___I liked English and social studies in school.

7.___I would call myself expressive.

8.___I cherished my books when I was young.

9.___I still cherish my books.

10.___I have written a story, poem, or manuscript because I enjoyed writing it.

Add the items you have checked: _____

Logical-Mathematical Intelligence

1.___As a child, I liked to put things together.

2.___I like math.

3.___I was more likely to play with blocks than recite nursery rhymes.

4.___I watch scientific television shows and movies and/or keep current on scientific discoveries.

continued on next page

STEP **8**

5.___People say I'm very logical.

6.___Sometimes I am critical of others' logic.

7.___I can count in my head.

8.___I am intrigued by mathematical formulas.

9.___I like playing games that involve solving problems.

10.___I believe that anything worthwhile can be explained.

Add the items you have checked: _____

Spatial Intelligence

1.___When I was young, I liked puzzles.

2.___I rarely need to ask for directions.

3.___I'm good at reading charts and graphs.

4.___I can see colors and images in my head.

5.___I doodle, draw, and scribble at times.

6.___I enjoy taking pictures.

7.___Geometry wasn't hard for me in school.

8.___I easily recognize faces.

9.___I remember details.

10.___I admire people who are good chess players.

Add the items you have checked: _____

Bodily-Kinesthetic Intelligence

1.___I think better when I am moving around.

2.___I am a born "ham" and love to perform.

3.___I like to get on the playing field, run, walk, or do other physical activity.

4.___I often touch things to see how they feel.

5.___To learn something new, I have to do it, not read about it.

6.___I have good eye–hand coordination.

7.___I enjoy doing two things at once.

8.___I like working with my hands.

9.___People say I talk with my hands.

10.___I have an ability to handle objects with skill and grace.

Add the items you have checked: _____

STEP **8**

Musical Intelligence

1.___I listen to music whenever I can.

2.___I like to sing, tap out rhythms, and hum.

3.___I remember jingles and television commercials with music.

4.___I play musical instruments.

5.___Often I have a song or melody in my head.

6.___I have a good ear for nonverbal sounds.

7.___I have written songs or changed the words to familiar songs.

8.___Music makes me come alive.

9.___I loved music when I was a child.

10.___I can hear a song once or twice and remember it.

Add the items you have checked: _____

Interpersonal Intelligence

1.___When I was a child, I could talk with people of all ages.

2.___I was a leader at a young age.

3.___I am able to help people solve disputes.

4.___I "read" people easily.

5.___People have said that I am compassionate and kind.

6.___I like working as a group.

7.___People often feel comfortable telling me about personal and professional concerns.

8.___I am good at teaching.

9.___I often participate in groups outside of work.

10.___I consider my friendships very special.

Add the items you have checked: _____

Intrapersonal Intelligence

1.___I am very aware of what I am feeling and thinking.

2.___I know my strengths and weaknesses.

3.___People have always considered me independent.

4.___I enjoy doing things alone.

5.___I have attended educational seminars on personal growth.

6.___The prospect of going to a party doesn't thrill me.

continued on next page

STEP **8**

7.___I am in my own business or have thought about it.

8.___I like my personal space.

9.___I can be content sitting and thinking about things.

10.___I engage in activities outside of work mostly on my own.

Add the items you have checked: _____

Naturalist Intelligence

1.___I like to classify different plants and animals.

2.___I like to spend time outdoors in natural environments.

3.___I like to take care of animals.

4.___I enjoy gardening.

5.___I interact with things in the environment.

6.___I enjoy watching nature.

7.___When I am in a car, I pay attention to natural surroundings.

8.___If I could, I would work in the natural environment rather than an office.

9.___Using a microscope appeals to me.

10.___I like to visit zoos and botanical gardens.

Add the items you have checked: _____

How to Teach or Learn Anything Eight Different Ways

To accommodate different intelligences, theorists propose eight different potential pathways to learning. Learning style is important in customer service from the standpoint of teaching your customers. Not all customers learn in the same way. To get your point across, you may need to draw a map for someone who is confused about oral directions. Or you might need to draw a picture of the kind of product you are explaining. If someone does not understand how to put merchandise together from the instructions provided, you may need to show him. If you are having difficulty reaching a customer, the theory of multiple intelligences suggests

STEP **8**

several ways in which the material might be presented to facilitate effective learning. See if the customer connects with

- **Words** (linguistic intelligence)
  Explain in words, a quick poem if you can make one up, analogies, conversation.
- **Numbers or logic** (logical-mathematical intelligence)
  Show the advantages in cost, savings, discounts on number of items.
- **Pictures** (spatial intelligence)
  Show pictures of the product, how people use it, what it looks like, what each step looks like when you put it together.
- **A physical experience** (bodily-kinesthetic intelligence)
  Let the customer touch the item, play with the toy or game if they are buying for a child or if they are a child.
- **Music** (musical intelligence)
  Have music playing in your booth or office. Research shows that customers retain more when music is playing, and that it increases endorphins and just plain makes people happy.
- **A social experience** (interpersonal intelligence)
  Ask someone else to come over and discuss the purchase so more interaction can take place.
- **Self-reflection** (intrapersonal intelligence)
  Have them think about how they would use the merchandise, how they would feel about it in their home, what they think would be good about the purchase.
- **An experience in the natural world** (naturalist intelligence)
  Take a walk with the customer if that is permitted, go outside to the patio, reference the outdoors, the environment, and natural products.

To find your style, complete Worksheet 8.2 or visit www.edutopia.org/multiple-intelligences-introduction.

STEP **8**

You don't have to teach or learn something in all eight ways, just see what the possibilities are and then decide which particular pathways interest you the most, or seem to be the most effective teaching or learning tools. Use the technique of Mind Mapping to discover how you might integrate multiple intelligences when instructing customers. Dr. Thomas Armstrong, educator and psychologist in the field of multiple intelligences, suggests a Mind Mapping exercise on his website to get started.

> Put the topic of whatever you're interested in teaching or learning about in the center of a blank sheet of paper, and draw eight straight lines or "spokes" radiating out from this topic. Label each line with a different intelligence. Then start brainstorming ideas for teaching or learning that topic and write down ideas next to each intelligence (this is a spatial-linguistic approach of brainstorming; you might want to do this in other ways as well, using a tape-recorder, having a group brainstorming session, and so on). Have fun! (www.thomasarmstrong.com/multiple_intelligences.htm)

For more information on how to create Mind Maps, visit www.imindmap.com or review Tony Buzan and Richard Israel's book, *Brain Sell* (1996).

You should now be armed with lots of tools and many new ideas to think about when working with customers. Hopefully, you also gained some insight into how you learn and what style of teaching you prefer.

One more note about teaching customers. It is important to know how much a customer knows about your area or product.

- If a customer knows very little, instruct a lot, go slowly, step by step, and get confirmation with each step that the customer understands.
- If a customer knows a little, instruct, praise each step of knowledge she demonstrates to you, and let her know that confusion is normal and will dissipate when she learns more and does more.

♦ If a customer is unsure, coach and let him know he can do whatever it takes to use your product, and reinforce his self-esteem and confidence.

♦ If a customer wants to do it herself, honor her wishes and be there to provide any assistance she requests.

Enjoy your customers!

♦ ♦ ♦

Put It All Together

Customers come in all different sizes, shapes, and personalities. Step 8 gave you tools to understand their differences and become aware of personality and learning types that will help you respond to a variety of behaviors. Step 9 will help you identify what annoys you, for the purpose of allowing you to think before you respond. Negotiating tips are also covered in this step, as well as ways to help diffuse difficult situations and people.

STEP 8

STEP
8

Keep It Cool When Things Get Hot

After all you've tried and all you've done, after all you've "given" and all you have endured, it's still possible that there's a customer or two who just drive you up a wall. It may seem that no matter what you do, nothing will please them.

There is no way you will be able to please everyone 100 percent of the time. This is just a fact. However, you will be able to please most people, and if you know a few tips about how to work with customers who get angry, you might even be able to please the few people who seem unreachable.

What Pushes Your Buttons?

If someone were to "come at you" with a clenched fist, clearly about to hit you, what would you do? You would prepare for the fight. You would get ready to hit the person back, run, or act in whatever way you perceived to be self-preserving.

TOOL 9.1

Behaviors that Push Buttons

Lying	Shouting	Breaking lines
Cursing	Answering cell phones	Impatience
Inconsideration	Power plays	Disrespect
Automated phones	People who don't listen	Complainers
Last-minute customers	Rude people	Self-important people
Arrogance	Dishonesty	Control freaks
Aggressive people	Irresponsibility	Tattle-tales
Rigidity	Bossy people—do it now!	Flakey people
Manipulative people	Passive-aggressive behavior	Loud talkers
People who are insulting	Slackers	Hot heads
People in denial	Threats	Demands

Similarly, if a customer pushes your buttons, you react. "Pushing buttons" means that somebody does something that causes you to have a visceral response. It doesn't have to be as serious as threatening to hit you. It could be cursing. It could be lying. It could be any number of things. For each person, what pushes your buttons is personal, and often has to do with your beliefs and values.

Tool 9.1 describes some behaviors and characteristics that people have found offensive. See if any of them push your buttons too.

You can and do deal with minor provocations on a daily basis. But, behaviors that really bother you can be your nemesis. Once you identify behaviors that you can't tolerate, you will find that bringing them to the foreground will give you a better chance of overcoming the effect they have on you. Working through conflicts that occur because someone has pushed your buttons will be

WORKSHEET 9.1

What Pushes Your Buttons?

What Pushes Your Buttons?	How Do People Usually Respond to Your Behavior?	How Would You Like to React?

productive for you professionally. This is true for interactions with staff members and bosses as well as customers. Refer to Worksheet 9.1 to determine what pushes your buttons and how you would prefer to respond.

Recognize the Stages of Rage

Some customers have built-up emotions before they even get to you and have "war stories." For example, they accessed your website and had to go through contortions to figure out instructions. They called and were transferred to six people. They had to come to your facility in person. The receptionist was rude. She gave them the wrong floor. Now they are on the right floor, in front of you.

STEP
9

TOOL 9.2

Stages of Rage

1. They feel powerless. Nothing they have tried worked.
2. They feel frustrated.
3. They become enraged.

People actually go through stages on their way to rage. Keep the points in Tool 9.2 in mind. If you consider that there are prescribed ways that people react, it will help you not take their disappointment and anger personally.

Of course, it is best to resolve a problem before anyone gets enraged. By the time someone gets to the third stage of rage, you have to deal with the drama in addition to solving the actual problem. Rage is often characterized by raised voices, seething, and irrational thinking. When anger ensues, adrenaline kicks in and continues to pump until the person calms down. As we have said before, the worst thing to say is "calm down." But, calming down is what you have to wait for in order to proceed with the transaction.

When a customer is in a stage of rage, avoid judging, criticizing, blaming, jumping to conclusions, assuming, getting angry yourself, arguing, interrupting, acting like you already know what the speaker is saying, acting disinterested, tuning out, faking attention, doing something else, misinterpreting, or thinking of what you are going to say next. Let the person wind down. Help by understanding and showing that you care. Review the following techniques and practice active listening.

Demonstrate Active Listening

◆ Stop what you are doing.
◆ Try to get the person to a comfortable area away from people.
◆ Establish and maintain eye contact.

- Project sincerity verbally and nonverbally.
- Repeat what the person is saying, or paraphrase.
- Ask open-ended and closed-ended questions.
- Respond with empathy for feelings and thoughts.
- Offer assistance.
- Show that you care.
- Apologize or express regret as appropriate.
- Come to a mutually agreeable solution.
- Verify the solution.
- Express support.

Practice Sorting

You also can choose to "sort" or ignore a statement that you don't want to address or a phrase that pushes your buttons. Sorting means that you make the choice to move on and disregard a comment, such as

- a personal attack
- sarcasm
- obvious exaggeration.

> **POINTER**
> Sorting is skipping over what was said and dealing only with the important issues. You may choose to go back to a comment that you have sorted at a time in the conversation when the person is not so upset.

Sorting is skipping over what was said and dealing only with the important issues. You may choose to go back to a comment that you have sorted at a time in the conversation when the person is not so upset.

Use "I" Statements

Tony: "Hello, may I help you?"

Orlando: "I doubt it. I feel like I've been on a roller coaster with you people, and it won't stop. If I have to be bumped around anymore, I'm going to scream!"

Tony: "I'm disappointed that we haven't been able to help you. Maybe I can do better today."

Orlando: "If you don't fix my cable, I'm going to sue you."

STEP 9

Tony: "I can tell you are angry. Tell me what happened.
          Give me a chance to help."

In the previous scenario, Tony chose to ignore sarcasm and threats in favor of getting to the point. He also used "I" statements, taking personal responsibility to assist. When a staff member or a manager uses "I," it changes the interaction to a personal promise or a personal commitment, such as "I will help you." Using "I" or "me" statements like those in Tool 9.3 helps build trust.

"I" statements are also used in communication when you have feedback to give and you want to avoid conflict by not blaming but, rather, by taking responsibility for what you want.

TOOL 9.3

Assertive "I" Statements

"I can help you."

"Let me help you."

"It would help me if we could figure this out together."

"I need you to . . . "

The University of Colorado Conflict Resolution Consortium provides the following description and example of "I" statements on its website:

> I-messages or I-statements are a way of communicating about a problem to another person without accusing them of being the cause of the problem. Often, when someone has a problem with another person, they tell him or her so by using a "you-statement," for example, "you didn't finish the financial report on time!" While that statement may be true, by phrasing it that way, the listener is likely to get defensive and begin to argue. For instance, he might reply, "I couldn't because the deadline was unreasonable!" or "You are always pestering me. I'd get more done if you'd just leave me alone!"

Another approach to the same problem is using an "I-message." For example, the worker could say, "I really am getting backed up on my work since I don't have the financial report yet." The coworker's response to this statement is likely to be more conciliatory. For example, she might respond, "I know. I'm sorry. I'll finish it up today and try harder to meet my deadlines. I had a lot of things piling up at once this week, but I'll get it to you as quickly as I can." While this doesn't completely solve the problem, it retains the good working relationship between the two people, and is more likely to generate more cooperative interactions in the future than the accusatory "you message" approach. (www.colorado.edu/conflict/peace/treatment/istate.htm)

Dealing with Difficult People

Tool 9.4 offers tips for dealing with people who demonstrate the behaviors that many find offensive. In addition to the tips, there are also ways that you can help yourself cope with negativity. Unfortunately, you can't always change someone else's behavior. You can, however, modify your own reactions, behaviors, and even feelings.

Create Ways to Cope

There are ways to help you overcome the effects of difficult personal interactions. To keep your wits about you, it's important to release the tension that you are holding inside. It is normal and natural to have feelings when you are confronted with anger, resentment, disappointment, and antagonism. Learning new skills for reframing how you view situations will help.

STEP **9**

TOOL 9.4

Responding to Difficult People

Behavior	Response
Rude, arrogant, and loud	**Be assertive.** Don't fight. Do not back away. Speak in a clear and audible voice. State your opinion or action with authority.
Sarcasm	**Ask what the person means.** If someone is taking "pot shots" behind someone else's back, ask the speaker to say what he or she means, and to speak directly with the person they are attacking. Ask for the truth instead of sarcasm, i.e., "Did you really mean that her report was a travesty?"
Complaining	**Help solve the problems without agreeing with the complainer.** (Agreeing with people reinforces their behavior.) Understand, and encourage action.
Silent	**Ask open-ended questions.** Use a "silent stare." Make sure your body language is receptive and open. Listen to responses.
Negative—think people in power can't be trusted	**Be optimistic.** Give alternate opinions and examples.
Over-committers	**Help them "chunk" their activities into manageable pieces.** Give them deadlines that include dates to submit in the middle of the project as well as at the end.

Use Journals to Write

Other ways for you to keep your cool include writing your thoughts down and talking to others who understand what you are experiencing. Journals can be used in two ways:

1. You can document what happened and how it was resolved. Documenting what occurred helps keep the facts straight. It also allows you to get your thoughts down

on paper and out of your immediate focus. Moreover, documenting the facts may be useful, should you ever need to explain what happened.

2. Use writing to vent. When you are venting, you can say anything. You can use the technique of answering the following:

   a. What I'd like to say to . . . (customer, colleague, employee)

   b. What I'd like to say to me . . . (what reinforcement you would like to give yourself)

When you use the second technique, it would be wise to take your journal home with you. Your intentions may be misunderstood if someone were to read it.

Find Allies

Don't assume that everyone is against you. Check your perceptions. Gain support for you as a person and a professional. Often, someone you find is difficult is also difficult for others. Without gossiping, notice how others respond to the person who annoys you, and check your perceptions with them. Take comfort in the knowledge that it's "not just you."

Develop a Mantra

A mantra is a phrase that you say over and over again. It solidifies a sound in your mind, and it is a way to relieve stress because it is repetitive. Saying a mantra over and over pushes other thoughts out of your mind. Your mantra might say: "I know I can handle this . . . I know I can handle this . . . " Or, for relaxation, you can just repeat an "hmm" or another sound.

STEP 9

Use Assertive Language

You don't always need to sort comments. You may want to address some rude behavior head on. Be assertive, but not aggressive or rude yourself. Statements like those in Tool 9.5 may help you get started.

TOOL 9.5

Assertive Statements

"Time out! I want to hear what you're saying, but I've got to ask you to slow down a bit."

"Let's talk about this. You go first and I won't interrupt you. Then when you're done, I'll see if I have any questions."

"I will respect your opinion. I need you to respect my opinion as well."

Sometimes you need to give feedback to a staff member, a peer, or a customer. There is a rule for giving feedback that is important: If you don't have a positive reason for giving feedback, don't give it.

POINTER

If you don't have a positive reason for giving feedback, don't give it.

If someone cannot change his or her behavior, or if you are angry and want to "get back" at someone, consider whether your feedback will cause a positive result. If not, it might be best to wait and rethink what you would like to convey. When you are ready, focus on the situation, not the person. Feedback is about behavior, not what you think of the person's character or characteristics. Give examples of what you have observed, and how it affected you or your team. Keep the examples to one issue.

When you give feedback, it is not a time to reveal all the concerns you have had that you never addressed. It should be short and timely, when it happens or within the day: "I noticed that you came in late. This put the team in a bind because we needed to review your part of the agenda first." Ask the other person for his or her response to your feedback. A rule of thumb is to ask the person what she thinks within four seconds. This avoids a long and drawn out explanation. ("And not only that . . . you didn't give me the report due last week, and you didn't make the meeting two weeks ago. I can't depend on you anymore.") When the person

STEP **9**

gives you an explanation, say what you need, and come to consensus on the solution. ("If you are going to be late, please call. Will you be able to do that in the future?") Then appreciate the person for resolving the issue. ("Thanks. I know that we will be able to count on you.")

Keep in mind that feedback is not corrective action, although, corrective action does involve feedback.

The Negotiating Process

Whether you are negotiating for yourself or to help others come to agreement, give and take is required to unveil the issues or motivations. Negotiating can yield a better outcome than you expected if you are open to discussing alternatives and points of view. Follow the Five Steps for Negotiation in Tool 9.6 for ways that will help the negotiations yield positive results.

Remember:
- You are not a pushover.
- You are professional.
- You are calm enough to respond to the person's anger.
- You are a good negotiator.
- You can focus on what is important.
- You are capable.

◆ ◆ ◆

Put It All Together

Button pushers often cause us to react. If you know what you are most likely to react to, you can stop an interaction from escalating and work through issues to make the situation productive. When all is said and done, customer service begins and ends with you. Step 10 provides suggestions for keeping physically and mentally healthy, and honors you.

TOOL 9.6

Five Steps to Successful Negotiating

> Step 1: Go to the balcony.

> Step 2: Stay on topic.

> Step 3: Acknowledge the elephant in the room.

> Step 4: Move parties from where they are to where they can be.

> Step 5: Give them a bridge over which to retreat.

1. **Go to the balcony.** As conflict unfolds, remember that you are the steward in the discussion. In your mind, go above the conflict and watch from the balcony. Pretend it's only a movie. Who are the people in conflict? What do they really want? Watch the characters and learn from the clues what each person wants.

2. **Stay on topic.** As often as needed, bring the discussion back to the main issue(s). Clarify the concerns and the points. Keep people from expanding on the scope of the disagreement. Stick to the topic for a solution. Be the owner of the conversation and stay on track.

3. **Acknowledge the elephant in the room.** If there is something that people are *not* saying, and you know that it is relevant to the conflict, call it out. Speak the words that everyone else can't say. There is a magic to speaking aloud something that others are saying to themselves. When it's uncovered, people can deal with it.

4. **Move parties from where they are to where they can be.** Each person has unique values and strengths, and each person views the conflict from a different context. Conflict can create great innovation. For you as a negotiator, you will need to listen deeply to each of the players and understand his or her unique viewpoint. Only then can you determine how far each person is willing to move. You may need to take a break to figure out your strategy.

5. **Give them a bridge over which to retreat.** When someone refuses to collaborate, no matter what anyone says or does, it generally doesn't mean that he or she is ignorant of the logic of the points being expressed; it means he or she is resisting. Give the person a way to retreat safely. Try to come up with a way to make it seem like the solution was his or her idea. Find a way for the resister to agree and save face. Take the time that is needed to work through the conflict productively.

(Adapted from *10 Steps to Successful Project Management*, Lou Russell, 2007, American Society for Training & Development)

Be Your Own Best Customer

OVERVIEW

You are the most important customer

Take care of yourself

Avoid worry and catastrophizing

Appreciate the good and contemplate altruism

Take a moment to consider what makes you happy outside of work. What activities, people, and events contribute to your happiness? Work is just one aspect of your life that could (and should) give you some pleasure.

Complete Worksheet 10.1. This exercise gives you a chance to identify, remember, or imagine activities that you find pleasurable. People sometimes deny themselves simple pleasures because they think

- ◆ I'm too busy.
- ◆ Others need me.
- ◆ I don't deserve time to myself.
- ◆ I was taught to always do things for other people.
- ◆ I feel guilty when I take time away from my family.
- ◆ I feel guilty when I am not doing something "productive."
- ◆ I have to please the people who are important to me before I can take care of myself.

STEP 10

WORKSHEET 10.1
Ten Things I Like to Do

Things I Like to Do	Last Time I Did It	When I Will Do It
1.		
2.		
3.		
4.		
5.		
6.		
7.		
8.		
9.		
10.		

You Are the Most Important Customer

You are important and just as deserving as your family and friends. When you complete Worksheet 10.1, you may realize how long it's been since you actually did some of the things you really like to do, just for you and not for anyone else (unless you need a partner to do it). This could be going to a concert, playing guitar, listening to music, playing softball, making love, skydiving, camping, riding a bike, talking to a friend, reading a novel, eating ice cream, going to a play, watching football, and so on. You also might discover that many of your activities don't cost anything, like taking a walk with someone you care about or visiting a park with the family. That's an added advantage.

STEP **10**

Several psychologists and spiritual authors have been referenced in this book, all of whom agree that the mind needs a rest from thinking every now and again. William Glasser (1976) ascribed to the concept of *positive addiction*, a term he used for an activity that strengthens us, makes our lives more satisfying, and puts us in a thought-free state. An example of this practice is the highs that runners get, which are said to be extremely healthy for the mind and the spirit. Glasser found that positive addiction to a sport or an activity increases self-confidence and the power of imagination. By doing something enjoyable, you can increase your mind's capacity without having to do anything you *don't* like to do. What a concept!

In *Happiness Now! Timeless Wisdom for Feeling Good Fast*, Robert Holden (2007) exposes myths about being happy, and examines assumptions that some people hold about thinking you have to suffer to be happy. See Worksheet 10.2 for ways that suffering is described. Complete this exercise to see how much suffering you do, whether it is intentional or unintentional.

Everyone has different ways of getting sane, staying sane, approaching sane, or appearing sane. You have good times and not-so-good times. The important thing is that you "don't let the turkeys get you down," and that you continue to create wellness and happiness in your life. The point of staying positive is to think about positive things, and not to dwell on negatives, as the Law of Attraction suggests.

Take Care of Yourself

The following suggestions apply to everyone. Try them and see if work gets better, customers don't seem as taxing, and companies don't seem as impersonal. Make your life personal.

See Your Friends

Friends help shape your identity. They make you laugh, ponder, reflect, and care. In the book *Best Friends* (Apter & Josselson, 1998),

WORKSHEET 10.2

Myths and Assumptions

Instructions: Check all that apply to you.

I believe:

	Yes	No
in order to experience enjoyment, you have to suffer first	❏	❏
work before pleasure is a must	❏	❏
you have to be productive all the time	❏	❏
vegging out is lazy	❏	❏
"the best things in life are free" is a hoax	❏	❏
everything has a cost	❏	❏

You are:

	Yes	No
harder on yourself than anyone else	❏	❏
often ill	❏	❏
uncomfortable with wealth and luxury	❏	❏
suspect of anything that comes easily	❏	❏

You feel guilty when:

	Yes	No
you relax	❏	❏
something comes your way without hard work	❏	❏
you are recognized for a skill or talent that comes easily to you	❏	❏
you say "no"	❏	❏

the authors have a statement about how friends listen to each other that is priceless: **"We learn how to listen each other into speech."**

When you listen to each other, you validate your worth and the worth of your friend. Even when you are with a friend in silence, or in an activity without words, you connect. You also don't have any hesitation in thinking a best friend is forever. Friends make sure you don't feel alone in the world, understand your peculiarities, and even express them with fond regard: "She doesn't do well with south, north, east, and west; just give her landmarks" or "He's not into ties, but his hats are a tribute to fashion."

STEP **10**

Real friends stand by you through thick and thin, good and bad, ups and downs, new loves and breakups, old girlfriends and boyfriends, kids and no kids, illness and health. The number one song requested from James Taylor when he was on Oprah Winfrey was "You've Got a Friend." Call a friend!

Give Yourself a Break

There used to be a McDonald's commercial that said, "Give yourself a break today . . . at McDonald's. We're all for you!" Hamburgers may not be the healthiest food in the universe, but giving yourself a break is good for your health.

I have mentioned Sid Simon several times in different steps. Sid had a saying: **"Remember that you are always doing the best you can."** You can go back and correct mistakes, or you can move on. It's a choice. Sid's point is that if you could do better, you would. At any given time, no matter what the circumstance, you are doing the best you can. This applies even if you think you aren't doing the best you can. There's a reason you aren't if that is the case. If you look at yourself in this light, you will not beat yourself up or contribute to eroding your self-esteem. If you want to do better the next time, plan how to do it.

Give Others a Break

There are reasons that people do not always live up to your expectations. Rather than fret over it, try to understand what might be happening, instead of judging, criticizing, gossiping, or responding in a negative way. There will always be actions that grate on you. Try to practice forgiveness. Your acceptance might come right back—remember reciprocity.

Avoid Worry and Catastrophizing

It's exhausting to worry. Catastrophizing is making a case for things to get worse and worse. It's looking at a hangnail and

WORKSHEET 10.3

What Makes You Happy?

Instructions: Check off items that apply to you. In the second column, describe how it works or doesn't work for you.

In order to be happy, I must	If this doesn't work, what would you change?
❑ Be liked by everyone	
❑ Be right all the time	
❑ Be competent at all I do	
❑ Never get frustrated	
❑ Always be good	
❑ Always be in control	
❑ Always be calm	
❑ Avoid conflict	
❑ Wait for happiness to happen	
❑ Be treated fairly by everyone	
❑ Overcome my past	
❑ Deserve it	
❑ Never get angry	
❑ Be perfect	
❑ Be on time	
❑ Never let down my guard	
❑ Hide my feelings	
❑ Never be vulnerable	
❑ Have a partner	
❑ Weigh less	
❑ Have more muscle tone	
❑ Have a smaller stomach	
❑ Exercise more	

STEP **10**

In order to be happy, I must	If this doesn't work, what would you change?
☐ Get a face-lift	
☐ Eat less	
☐ Look like a model	

thinking you have cancer. It's having an argument and tormenting yourself that your forever friendship is over. It's making a mountain out of a molehill. It's worrying that someone has been in an accident when he or she is five minutes late. You can eliminate catastrophizing by staying in present time. If you do not project into the future and hypothesize about the past, you can stop yourself from unnecessary anxiety. Worrying about something will not change it. Complete Worksheet 10.3 to find out what makes you happy and why. If you need to change your mindset, answering the following questions may give you an insight into stress that you may be creating for yourself.

Answer these questions:
◆ What are you telling yourself that is making you anxious?
◆ What are the facts?
◆ What are possible alternative reasons for what you are observing?
◆ How many times has your catastrophizing come true?
◆ How is worrying affecting you?

Try these steps:
◆ Do something positive.
◆ Change your scenery.
◆ Take a walk.
◆ Focus on the present.

For more ideas, see www.moodletter.com/NegativeSelfTalk.htm.

STEP 10

TOOL 10.1

Take Risks

◆ Once you decide to take action, go forward with your plans.

◆ Be fully committed to what you are doing.

◆ Ask for what you want.

◆ Consider what you think more than what others will think.

◆ Focus on your goals, not your "image."

◆ Practice risk taking.

Take Risks

Taking risks increases self-esteem. Think about a time when you have taken risks. How did it work out? Have you changed jobs? Bought a home? Presented in front of a group? Taking risks changes your perspective. Consider the actions in Tool 10.1 for encouragement.

Express Yourself

It takes courage to express your point of view. Like taking risks, expressing yourself builds confidence. It also lets others know where you stand. When you respect yourself enough to let people know who you are, others will respect your courage.

Allow for Flexibility

Even when you plan, life happens. If you view changes in plans as opportunities to grow, you will be less likely to be stressed by the unexpected. There will never be a time when all things will go as smoothly as you would like, so why not develop ways that you can anticipate and accept change and alleviate as many downsides of the disruption as you can?

STEP **10**

Exercise

Exercise increases endorphins and has innumerable positive effects on your heath. Do something you enjoy. Dance, play ping-pong, swim, walk, run, participate in sports with children, or participate in competitive sports. A personal trainer or doctor can advise you of the best course of action for your body and health. Exercise should have some element of fun, even if it's merely the satisfaction you get out of doing it.

You can exercise in the office or on break. You can walk, do simplified yoga, raise your arms and lower them, move your head from side to side, rotate one shoulder at a time and then both shoulders, and stretch. Deep breathing is also a way to relax. Breathe in deeply; hold it for ten seconds, then breath out. Repeat three to five times.

Get Proper Nutrition

Proper nutrition means different things to different people. Whether you are a carnivore, a vegetarian, or a vegan, nutrition is important. Make sure you are getting all the nutrients you need from your meals and snacks. Some nutritionists believe that you should eat five small meals a day to keep your energy up and your sugar stabilized, assuming you don't have a lot of sugar in your meals or snacks. Talk to your doctor to determine what is best for you.

Appreciate the Good

There are many good things that you enjoy in life, including many good customers. Using Worksheet 10.4 as a reference, make a list of the good things you have, and read the list in the morning before you go to work. Share the list with the good people you have referenced on the list. Share good things with your family or team, and have family members and team members do the same.

WORKSHEET 10.4

It's All Good

I think about what is good in my life.

I appreciate what I have.

I appreciate me.

I appreciate my friends.

I appreciate my family.

I minimize what I have no power to change.

I like who I am.

I have an activity that I enjoy outside of work.

I take quiet time when I want or need it.

I relax.

I have fun.

I have people I trust with whom I can share thoughts.

I express my emotions to friends, family, and others as appropriate.

I am confident.

Contemplate Altruism

Altruism is a concept in philosophy and psychology that is defined as unselfish regard for or devotion to the welfare of others.

Although reciprocity exists conceptually and practically, altruism has benefits that are rewarding. You can give of yourself at work. You can give to charitable causes. You can volunteer. Nobody can tell a person to be altruistic. But, since much has been said in this book about feeling good, consider doing something kind without hesitation, surprising someone with kindness, or establishing a connection. You probably do that all the time without the suggestion being made. If you do, appreciate yourself for it. Surely others will.

As Wayne Dyer (1983) said in *Gifts From Eykis*:

Learn to cultivate your own garden.

The kingdom of heaven is within.

Everything in the universe is exactly as it should be.

It's never too late to have a happy childhood.

Keep it simple.

These are the good old days.

You are perfect.

Conclusion

Marcus Buckingham is an advocate of the "strengths revolution." In his books, *Now, Discover Your Strengths* and *Go Put Your Strengths to Work* and *The Truth About You*, Buckingham tackles questions such as, "What would happen if 75 percent of the day, you were using your strongest skills and engaged in your favorite tasks, doing exactly what you wanted to do?"

In a YouTube presentation (www.youtube.com/watch?v=wuZBJQAFOfM), the author talks about his mission: helping people put their strengths and passions to work, so people can have a chance to contribute and express the best of themselves, and to experience the satisfaction and success that practicing their passion brings.

Step 1 of this book addressed a similar theme. Worksheets were designed to uncover your skills, abilities, and hidden talents, and to encourage you to think about "the best you, the person you want to be." The take-away message in *10 Steps to Successful Customer Service* is to use your strengths and talents in your *present job* as well as keeping an eye to the future. With some thought and reflection, you can enjoy the position you hold. The Law of Attraction says that if you see the positive, you will get more positive.

In addition, putting your enhanced skills into practice may result in a promotion, what often occurs when heightened awareness and new behaviors are noticed. That would be terrific! And, as a part of the strengths revolution, you will be more aware of the strengths of others, and more prepared to coach and bring out their best. Alternatively, you may choose to move on to a different position, or to start your own business. Your enhanced skills will serve you no matter where you decide to offer your strengths.

In the YouTube video cited previously, Marcus Buckingham makes this comment: **"Work can be a great place where you can be challenged and you can make the kind of difference that only *you* can make."**

This is true. You are unique. You can make a distinctive difference.

May you be happy, healthy, and successful in all your endeavors.

Creating and Supporting a Customer Service Culture

The skills in *10 Steps to Successful Customer Service* need to be practiced by everyone from the frontline to the executive suite. Positive interactions are essential for excellent service, and outstanding customer service skills must be practiced by all staff members to achieve successful results. That is why *10 Steps to Customer Service* is geared to all levels. Everyone can improve interpersonal skills.

In addition to the contributions that each person makes, there are systematic customer-friendly procedures and processes that need to be implemented to ensure that the corporate or organizational culture supports internal and external customers. Tool A.1 includes areas to address for best customer service practices. For more examples, see the Balanced Scorecard at www. balancedscorecard.org. This approach allows companies to view all areas of the business for synergy. Vision, mission, and core values are usually addressed first, with goals, objectives, and action plans following in each of the areas in Tool A.1.

TOOL A.1

Creating and Supporting a Customer Service Culture

Financial
- ◆ Enough resources are provided to serve the customer, including staff, merchandise, food, and space.
- ◆ Costs to the customer are competitive; lower costs are explored and implemented.
- ◆ Financial rewards are given for customer satisfaction, including bonuses, trips, use of company vehicles, tickets to events, music, books, gift certificates, and special activities.
- ◆ All staff members are empowered with a certain amount of money they can use to "recover" or do something special for customers.
- ◆ Employees are compensated fairly with salaries and benefits.
- ◆ The company maintains effective financial controls and stays within budget.
- ◆ Employees recommend ways to save money and to innovate.

Customer Focus
- ◆ Leaders practice the courage of conviction and a profound customer focus.
- ◆ Practices put at least as much attention on internal customers as they do on external customers.
- ◆ Decisions are based on making a difference to the customer.
- ◆ Customer needs and behaviors are examined, monitored, and reported in a variety of ways and methods.
- ◆ As much attention is paid to customer satisfaction and loyalty as to financial measures.
- ◆ Employees are hired for their passion about customers.
- ◆ Conflicts are addressed internally and externally.
- ◆ Company perception is addressed.
- ◆ Employees are asked about their opinions of service on a regular basis.
- ◆ Teams invent ways that customers can experience new and different experiences.
- ◆ Everyone in the organization takes personal responsibility for providing an excellent customer experience.
- ◆ Leaders act as role models.
- ◆ Customer service triumphs are celebrated.

Tool A.1, continued

Growth and Learning	◆ Staff members are given information about the company, how it operates, and how all processes fit together to produce results for customers.
	◆ All staff is equipped with the training, tools, and skills needed to create customer loyalty.
	◆ Research is conducted, including interviewing leading subject matter customer service experts and reviewing articles, books, white papers, and best practices by other companies.
	◆ Team learning is essential. Members know how to cross-function with their team and with others in the organization. Opportunities exist to cross-train in a variety of ways with different departments.
	◆ Supervisors, managers, directors, and executives take advantage of learning opportunities to hone skills in leading, motivating, providing recognition, and contributing to process improvement.
	◆ The company recruits and hires people who are committed to customer service.
	◆ Developing employees is a priority.
	◆ Strengths are emphasized.
	◆ Gaps in skills are addressed through training and development.
	◆ Coaching and mentoring take place at all levels.
Business Processes and Technology	◆ Technology is easy for internal and external customers to use.
	◆ Websites, blogs, and electronic information are easy to read, easy to access, and clear.
	◆ Online ordering is simple.
	◆ There are several quick ways to reach company representatives.
	◆ Processes are customer focused.
	◆ Policies and procedures are customer friendly, such as return policies, discounts, and refunds.
	◆ Technology is constantly improved for internal and external customer ease and use, and for relevance.
	◆ Metrics measure the right things.
	◆ Future needs are explored regularly and are part of the planning process.
	◆ Employees provide input on what is necessary to optimize work and production.
	◆ What the company advertises, it delivers.

Enjoy the Journey: Tool and Worksheet Roundup

Following is a roundup of the worksheets and tools presented in this book that will help individuals, leaders, and training professionals find new pathways to develop personally or develop others to be great customer service professionals. You can pick and choose among these to find the mix that is right for your purpose and the journey you wish to take. Enjoy.

Step	Activity	All Staff	Leaders	Trainers
1	**Tool 1.1: Criteria for Identifying a Value**	Use as a definition and examples of values.	Use as a definition and examples of values.	Use as a definition and examples of values.
1	**Tool 1.2: Mission Statement Tips**	Create your own mission statement.	Share mission statements and develop a mission statement with and for your team.	Discuss how each person's mission statement fits into the overall company mission.
1	**Worksheet 1.1: Your Job Satisfaction**	Use to address current job satisfaction and mentoring opportunities.	Use as a team exercise or one on one to discover what people like about their jobs and how they can contribute more.	Conduct as an icebreaker or an exercise to highlight job satisfaction and discuss how managers and peers can mentor.
1	**Worksheet 1.2: Your Skills and Abilities**	Complete individually to determine skills, abilities, and hidden talents.	Conduct as teambuilding exercise. Pair members of the team to review worksheet together. Allow time for each person to share discoveries.	Instruct the class to complete the worksheet in pairs. Discuss hidden talents and ways to use them.
1	**Worksheet 1.3: Checklist for Personal Values**	Determine your most important values.	Complete as a group teambuilding exercise. Share values and how values influence each team member's actions.	Discuss how values determine actions and how values affect interactions and leadership.
2	**Tool 2.1: Leadership for Customer Loyalty**	Respond with your reactions to the leadership in your company.	Ask each team member to give you one change they would like to see based on their reflection when completing the exercise.	Conduct this exercise with the leadership of the company. Create action plans for improvements.

Step	Activity	All Staff	Leaders	Trainers
2	Worksheet 2.1: Your View of Customer Expectations	Complete the worksheet for insight into customer expectations.	Determine how each member on your team defines customer expectations based on answers in the worksheet. Create a combined list with the team.	Determine how each person in the class defines customer expectations. If you have different functions represented, have cross-functional teams create a combined list.
2	Worksheet 2.2: Customer Expectations	Complete the worksheet.	As a team, discuss answers. Focus on reasoning when members respond, not right or wrong. Give the correct answers with explanations.	Pair participants for evaluating the worksheet. Review each question and answer. Use as a pre-test and a post-test for classes that you teach on customer service.
3	Tool 3.1: Potential Imbalances	Use for reference.	Use for reference.	Use for reference.
3	Worksheet 3.1: Principles and Findings about Reciprocity	Write your reactions to the statements. Examine how each principle affects your relationships with both internal and external customers.	Use all the questions or pick out a few statements for discussion. Ask the team to come up with ways to improve teamwork. Have members compliment or praise each other.	Examine each concept. For additional information on reciprocity, see Blau's *Exchange and Power in Social Life* (1986).
3	Worksheet 3.2: Act the Part	This exercise is for a team.	Conduct with your team.	Conduct in teams. Give prizes for the team that acts the song or phrase out the quickest.
4	Tool 4.1: Tips on Listening	Use for reference.	Use for reference.	Use for reference.

Step	Activity	All Staff	Leaders	Trainers
4	**Tool 4.2:** **Questioning**	Use for reference.	Use for reference.	Use for reference.
4	**Worksheet 4.1:** **What Makes You Feel Connected to People?**	Complete the exercise yourself, exploring what keeps you connected to people.	Discuss as a team. Ask members to validate others who make them feel connected by answering questions with team member examples.	Pair participants to discuss their responses.
4	**Worksheet 4.2:** **Feelings Inventory**	Complete the inventory yourself, making a list of internal and external customer feelings.	Brainstorm a list of feelings with your team.	In teams or as a whole class, list feelings that internal and external customers experience.
4	**Worksheet 4.3:** **Listening on Both Levels**	Paraphrase the statements.	Paraphrase statements as a team. Ask each member to write down his or her own statement and have a partner paraphrase. Or, ask a question that you would like answered and have each member answer with a partner paraphrasing. Discuss.	Ask for examples of paraphrasing and empathizing from participants' responses. Conduct role plays with pairs. Have partners paraphrase each other's scenarios.
4	**Worksheet 4.4:** **Noise Detector Assessment**	Take the assessment.	After each member completes the assessment, ask people to share one strength and one growth opportunity with the team.	Pair participants to discuss their answers. Ask for volunteers to present strengths and opportunities for growth.
5	**Tool 5.1:** **Positive Language**	Use for reference.	Use for reference.	Use for reference.

Step	Activity	All Staff	Leaders	Trainers
5	**Tool 5.2:** A Dozen Musts for Phone Communication	Use for reference.	Use for reference.	Use for reference.
5	**Worksheet 5.1:** Negative to Positive	Complete the worksheet.	Share examples.	After people do the exercise individually, have teams place the best responses on a flipchart and report out.
5	**Worksheet 5.2:** Positive Qualities	Complete the exercise by recording the positive qualities that you have. Post the list up.	Tape flipchart paper on the wall. Ask team members to write down positive qualities of their team members. Make sure that everyone has qualities listed. Write positive qualities on the chart for all your team members and yourself.	Give each class member a piece of flipchart paper folded once or twice. Give tape for participants to tape the "capes" to their backs. Have people write positive qualities on the "capes."
5	**Worksheet 5.3:** The Power of a Positive Word	Follow the directions for the exercise.	This is a variation of Worksheet 5.2. Conduct with team members.	Conduct with class members.
6	**Tool 6.1:** Fantastic Service Equation	Use for reference.	Use for reference, discussion, and observation. Determine how the team can improve in each component.	Brainstorm how class members view the company's responsiveness in Fantastic Service Equation components.
6	**Tool 6.2:** FSET Survey— Fantastic Service Every Time	Complete survey.	Ask members what they do well and how they can improve.	Pair participants to discuss results of their own survey. Ask for volunteers to report a strength and an area to improve.

Step	Activity	All Staff	Leaders	Trainers
6	**Tool 6.3: Ways for Your Organization to Check Results**	Use for information.	Determine how your team presently uses data and new ways data could provide you with information.	Brainstorm ways the organization collects data and ways that might be useful. Report best practices from other companies.
6	**Worksheet 6.1: Identify Causes**	Complete the exercise yourself.	Complete the exercise with your team. Brainstorm how to avoid problems and solve common problems.	After participants complete the exercise, brainstorm how to avoid and solve problems that are common to class participants.
6	**Worksheet 6.2: Solve the Problem**	Solve a problem using the model.	Choose a problem that you would like the team to solve, or ask the team to identify a problem. Use the model to solve the problem. You may not be able to do it in one sitting.	In teams of no more than six, have participants choose a problem in each team, work through the model, and report their solutions to the rest of the class.
6	**Poem**	Read the poem. Create one yourself!	Create a team poem.	Have teams come up with their own poems and recite them to the class.
7	**Worksheet 7.1: Resolving Conflicts**	Complete exercise individually.	Compare individual answers to see if all team members have the same perception.	Discuss answers, taking into account that answers will be different for each operational area.
8	**Tool 8.1: Preferences—An Overview**	Use for reference.	Use for reference.	Use for reference.

Step	Activity	All Staff	Leaders	Trainers
8	Tool 8.2: Responding to Customer Types	Use for reference.	Use for reference.	Use for reference.
8	Worksheet 8.1: Different Customer Personalities	Complete the worksheet.	Discuss answers in your team and explore how customers might respond in your environment.	Discuss answers in pairs. Expand discussion to helping different customer types.
8	Worksheet 8.2: Smart Intelligence	Complete the worksheet.	Discuss individual results and how each person's intelligences contribute to the team.	Create teams by types of intelligence. Have teams discuss how different intelligences contribute in the workplace and report to class.
9	Tool 9.1: Behaviors that Push Buttons	Review to see if any behaviors push your buttons.	Use to review common button pushers.	Add additional behaviors with class.
9	Tool 9.2: Stages of Rage	Use for reference.	Use for reference.	Use for reference.
9	Tool 9.3: Assertive "I" Statements	Use for reference. Think of other statements that you could use.	Think of assertive statements as a team.	Brainstorm assertive statements.
9	Tool 9.4: Responding to Difficult People	Use as reference.	Use as reference.	Use as reference. Ask class to create examples or role plays.
9	Tool 9.5: Assertive Statements	Use as reference.	Use as reference.	Use as reference.

Step	Activity	All Staff	Leaders	Trainers
9	Tool 9.6: Five Steps to Successful Negotiating	Use as reference.	Discuss when you or people on the team have had to negotiate. Ask team members for examples. Take an example and use the process to discuss.	Team participants and have them identify a time when negotiating was necessary. Instruct teams to use the model to discuss and report their solutions to the class.
9	Worksheet 9.1: What Pushes Your Buttons?	Fill out the worksheet.	Discuss individual responses in the team with no judgment.	Have participants pair and discuss. Ask the group members what they learned.
10	Tool 10.1: Take Risks	Review the tool.	Ask team members to talk about the risks they take in the team or at work.	Review risk taking and its advantages. Ask what types of risks participants take at work and how they benefit from risk-taking.
10	Worksheet 10.1: Ten Things I Like to Do	Complete the worksheet.	Use as an icebreaker in a meeting.	Pair participants to discuss their lists.
10	Worksheet 10.2: Myths and Assumptions	Complete the worksheet.	Review concepts of "suffering."	Pair participants, or have them do the exercise silently. Discuss concepts as a summary.
10	Worksheet 10.3: What Makes You Happy?	Complete the worksheet.	Ask team members to discuss three items they learned.	Pair participants and ask them to discuss answers or three things they learned.
10	Worksheet 10.4: It's All Good	Complete the worksheet.	Ask team members to share what they choose.	Have participants share with each other.

REFERENCES

Apter, Terri, & Josselson, Ruthellen. *Best Friends*. Santa Clarita, CA: Crown Publishing, 1998.

Barlow, Jane, & Moller, Claus. *A Complaint is a Gift: Recovering Customer Loyalty When Things Go Wrong*. San Francisco: Berrett-Koehler, 2008.

Blackshaw, Pete. *Satisfied Customers tell Three Friends, Angry Customers Tell 3,000: Running a Business in Today's Consumer Driven World*. New York: Doubleday, 2008.

Blau, Peter. *Exchange and Power in Social Life*. New Brunswick, NJ: Transaction Publishers, 2008.

Brainy Quotes. Accessed February 16, 2009, from www.brainyquote.com/words/in/insolence179199.html.

Buckingham, Marcus, & Clifton, Donald. *Now, Discover Your Strengths*. New York, NY: The Free Press, 2001.

Buckingham, Marcus. *Go Put Your Stengths to Work: 6 Powerful Steps to Achieve Outstanding Performance*. New York: Simon & Schuster, 2007.

Buckingham, Marcus. *The Truth About You: Your Secret Success*. Nashville, TN: Thomas Nelson, 2008.

Buzan, Tony, & Israel, Richard. *Brain Sell: Harnessing the Selling Power of Your Whole Brain*. New York: McGraw-Hill, 1996.

Byrne, Rhonda. *The Secret*. Hillsborough, OR: Beyond Words Publishing, 2006.

Clark, Maxine, with Amy Joyner. *The Bear Necessities of Business: Building a Company with Heart*. Hoboken, NJ: John Wiley & Sons, Inc., 2006.

Dyer, Wayne. *Gifts From Eykis*. New York: Pocket Books, 1983.

Florida, Richard. *The Rise of the Creative Class*. New York: Basic Books, 2002.

Forum Corporation, Customer Experience Practice Team. "Uncommon Practice: What Leading Companies Do to Build Customer Loyalty." Boston: Forum Corporation, 2003.

Glasser, William. *Positive Addiction*. New York: Harper & Row, 1976.

Goodman, John. "The Truth According to TARP." *Competitive Advantage*. September, 2006.

Goodman, John. *Roadmaps for Delivering Winning Service: Customer Service Research Study*. Boston: Forum Corporation, 2003.

Gross, T. Scott. *Positively Outrageous Service*. New York: Warner Books, 1991.

Holden, Robert. *Happiness Now! Timeless Wisdom for Feeling Good Fast*. Carlsbad, CA: Hay House, 2007.

Kamin, Maxine. *Customer Service Training*. Alexandria, VA: American Society for Training and Development, 2006.

Migliani, Bob. *Treat Your Customers*. New York: Hyperion, 2006.

Naisbitt, John. *High Tech/High Touch: Technology and Our Accelerated Search for Meaning*. London, England: Nicholas Brealey Limited, 1999.

Naisbitt, John. *Megatrends*. New York: Warner Books, 1982.

Performance Research Associates. *Delivering Knock Your Socks Off Service*. New York: AMACOM, 2006.

Peters, Tom. *The Pursuit of Wow!* New York: Vintage Books, 1994.

Raths, Louis E., Harmin, Merrill, & Simon, Sidney B. *Values and Teaching: Working with Values in the Classroom*. Columbus, OH: Charles E. Merrill, 1966.

Russell, Lou. *10 Steps to Successful Project Management*. Alexandria, VA: American Society for Training & Development, 2007.

Smith, Maury. *A Practical Guide to Value Clarification*. University Associates, Inc.: La Jolla, California, 1977.

Senge, Peter. *The Fifth Discipline: The Art and Practice of the Learning Organization*. New York: Doubleday, 1990.

Willingham, Ron. *Integrity Service*. New York: Free Press, 2005.

I N D E X

Maxine Kamin, MEd, is a veteran trainer, educator, consultant, and administrator. After 14 years in academia, holding positions such as faculty member at the University of Massachusetts and acting dean of Instruction at Miami-Dade College, she followed her academic career with 20 years in business, education, and social service, including operating her own successful consulting firm full-time for 10 years, working as the manager of instruction and evaluation for American Express, and serving in her current position as director of Professional Development at ChildNet.

Ms. Kamin has worked with a variety of businesses and training organizations, including continuing education and corporate training departments at numerous colleges and universities. Her corporate clients include Fortune 500 companies, airports, hotels, stadiums, entertainment facilities, service organizations, call centers, financial institutions, and other industries. She has partnered with consulting firms including LORE International and Leadership International Management (LIM), and has held positions on boards including the Ft. Lauderdale chapters of the American Society for Training and Development and the Society for Human Resource Management.

In addition to being a consultant and trainer, Ms. Kamin is the author of *Customer Service Training*, one of ASTD's first "how to" books for trainers, and *Diversity Programs That Work*, an Info-Line publication that she coauthored with Cristina de Mello-e-Souza Wildermuth and Ron Collins. Some of her other training programs include Uncommon Courtesy, which is used in 36 states, Special Guests for the Florida Panthers, and Eleven Home Runs for Leadership. She is the curriculum designer for Positive Start, a supervisory training program that is now a three-credit college course, and part of the team that developed Supervising for Excellence, an intensive program for new supervisors in the field of child welfare.

As the founder and president of TOUCH Consulting, Inc.: *T*raining for *O*rganizational Development, *U*nparalleled *C*ustomer Service, Communications, and *H*uman Resources, headquartered in Plantation, Florida (www.touchconsulting.com), Ms. Kamin operates with the premise that the personal touch in business—respecting and appreciating associates and customers—is the key to success. Her programs are designed to give practical application to these principles.

^{THE} *ASTD* MISSION:

Through exceptional learning and performance, we create a world that works better.

The American Society for Training & Development provides world-class professional development opportunities, content, networking, and resources for workplace learning and performance professionals.

Dedicated to helping members increase their relevance, enhance their skills, and align learning to business results, ASTD sets the standard for best practices within the profession.

The society is recognized for shaping global discussions on workforce development and providing the tools to demonstrate the impact of learning on the organizational bottom line. ASTD represents the profession's interests to corporate executives, policy makers, academic leaders, small business owners, and consultants through world-class content, convening opportunities, professional development, and awards and recognition.

Resources
- *T+D (Training + Development)* Magazine
- ASTD Press
- Industry Newsletters
- Research and Benchmarking
- Representation to Policy Makers

Networking
- Local Chapters
- Online Communities
- ASTD Connect
- Benchmarking Forum
- Learning Executives Network

Professional Development
- Certificate Programs
- Conferences and Workshops
- Online Learning
- CPLP™ Certification Through the ASTD Certification Institute
- Career Center and Job Bank

Awards and Best Practices
- ASTD BEST Awards
- Excellence in Practice Awards
- E-Learning Courseware Certification (ECC) Through the ASTD Certification Institute

Learn more about ASTD at www.astd.org.
1.800.628.2783 (U.S.) or 1.703.683.8100
customercare@astd.org

080615.31410